Changing
Belief Systems
with NLP

by

Robert Dilts

Meta Publications
P. O. Box 565
Cupertino, California 95014

Library of Congress Card Number 90-060084
I.S.B.N. 0-916990-24-9

Contents

Dedication

This book is dedicated with deepest respect to the peoples of Eastern Europe who have shown the world the power and the reach of true belief change.

Acknowledgements

Credit History

There are a number of different elements in the creation and development of something, whether it be an object, theory, technique or idea. First of all, most products of creation have both a conceptual and operational side. The conceptual elements are the ideas that serve as the theoretical foundation of the product. The operational elements have to do with the implementation of ideas.

In terms of the conceptual and operational development there are a number of basic roles. There is the primary creator role which typically serves as the focal point for the development.

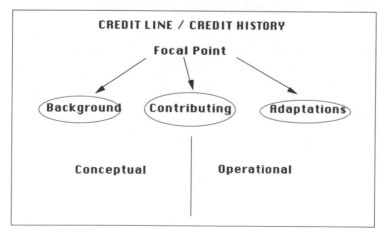

Then there is the conceptual and operational background support, contributing support and those who make further adaptations and refinements of the material.

While I served as the focal point for the development of the techniques described in this book, there are many people to acknowledge for their support roles.

For example, the technique of Reimprinting had both a conceptual and an operational history. Conceptually, **Reimprinting** is drawn from the background concept of "Imprinting" of **Konrad Lorenz,** which was extended to "re-imprinting" by **Timothy Leary.** It is also conceptually supported by **Sigmund Freud's** ideas from "Studies in Hysteria" and the family systems work of **Virginia Satir.** Operationally, however, Reimprinting is drawn primarily from the *Change history* technique of NLP developed by **Richard Bandler** and **John Grinder.**

The **Failure into Feedback** technique is primarily an extension of the work on accessing cues and cognitive strategies begun my colleagues and myself in the early days of NLP and described in the book *Neuro-Linguistic Programming Vol. I.* The innovative relational aspects of the process, however, were stimulated by the work of **Max Wertheimer** and his colleagues in the area of *Gestalt Psychology*.

The **Belief Integration** process draws operationally from a combination of the NLP techniques of the *Visual Squash* and *Reframing.* Conceptually, it has been heavily influenced by the work of **Fritz Perls** and **Virginia Satir.**

On a fundamental conceptual level, the notion of **Logical Levels** in belief change is drawn from **Gregory Bateson's** applications of logical levels in his studies of systems and schizophrenia. And much of the inspiration for the methods of applying these ideas was derived from the innovative work of **Milton H. Erickson, M.D.**

The physicalization of the **time-line** came from a series of innovations that arose out of a set of seminars I did with **John Grinder** called *Syntax,* as did the identification and physical changing of **perceptual positions** in the **Meta Mirror** technique.

A lot of incidental conceptual and operational support came from my colleague **Todd Epstein** who serves as the primary "beta test site" for many of my ideas.

On the production side of this book, many thanks go to **Louis Bellier** who transcribed and prepared the initial manuscript that served as the foundation for the book and **Alain Moenart** and **Anne Pierard** who sponsored the seminar from which the manuscript was drawn.

Introduction

Our beliefs are a very powerful force on our behavior. It is common wisdom that if someone really believes he can do something he will do it, and if he believes something is impossible no amount of effort will convince him that it can be accomplished. Beliefs like *"It's too late now;" "There's nothing I can do anyway;" "I'm a victim... My number came up;"* can often limit a person from taking full advantages of their natural resources and unconscious competence. Our beliefs about ourselves and what is possible in the world around us greatly impact our day-to-day effectiveness. All of us have beliefs that serve as resources as well as beliefs that limit us.

Most people recognize, for instance, that their belief systems can both directly and indirectly effect their health. It is often a simple matter to identify negative beliefs that lead to health related problems like substance abuse, constant fatigue, lowering of the body's natural defenses, and stress. Yet, how does one go about changing negative beliefs into beliefs that contribute to health?

Almost every health professional acknowledges that the attitude of the patient is a major contributing factor to the success of their recovery. Yet very few explicit or reliable methods exist to help someone get over their response of fear or apathy to achieve a congruent "positive attitude."

Throughout the history of medical research, placebos have been shown to be as powerful as many drugs. As yet, however, the exact cause of this power has remained a mystery. Many researchers speculate that a "reverse placebo effect" may even cause many cases of illness. Is it possible to tap into that power directly and channel it to insure successful recovery?

Even the beliefs that others have about us can effect us. This was demonstrated in an enlightening study in which a group of children who were tested to have average intelligence was divided at random into two equal groups. One of the groups was assigned to a teacher who was told that the children were "gifted." The other group was given to a teacher who was told that the children were "slow learners." A year later the two groups were retested for intelligence. Not surprisingly, the majority of the group that was arbitrarily identified as "gifted" scored higher than they had previously, while the majority of the group that was labeled "slow" scored lower! The teacher's beliefs about the students effected their ability to learn.

Our beliefs can shape, effect or even determine our degree of intelligence, health, relationships, creativity, even our degree of happiness and personal success. Yet, if indeed our beliefs are so powerful a force in our lives, how do we get control of them so they don't control us? Many of our beliefs were installed in us as children by parents, teachers, social upbringing and the media before we were aware of their impact or able to have a choice about them. Is it possible to restructure, unlearn or change old beliefs that may be limiting us and imprint new ones that can expand our potential beyond what we currently imagine? If so, how do we do it?

Neuro-Linguistic Programming (NLP) provides a powerful and exciting model of the mind and set of behavioral tools that can allow us to unlock some of the hidden mechanisms of beliefs and belief systems. Through the processes of NLP, beliefs and the neurolinguistic and physical elements which influence beliefs may be explored and influenced in a comprehensive and pragmatic way.

This book is a result of my own exploration of the underlying processes which influence beliefs using the tools of NLP. The book is primarily drawn from a manuscript of a seminar on belief change. By doing so I hope to present and preserve some of the feeling and interactive insight that comes from the real life experience of working with people and their beliefs.

Chapter I

The Nature of Belief

The brain, and in fact any biological or social system, is organized into levels. Your brain has different levels of processing. As a result you can have different levels of thinking and being. When we are working to understand the brain, or to change behaviors, we need to address these different levels. The same thing will be true inside a business system where there are different levels of organization.

From the psychological point of view there seem to be five levels that you work with most often. (1) The basic level is your *environment,* your *external constraints.* (2) You operate on that environment through your *behavior.* (3) Your behavior is guided by your mental maps and your strategies, which define your *capabilities:* (4) These capabilities are organized by *belief systems*—which are the subject of this work—and (5) beliefs are organized by *identity.*

So when a person is experiencing a difficulty, what you might want to know is whether this difficulty is coming from his external context,

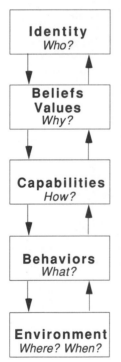

Figure 1. Logical Levels of Organization in Systems

or is it that he doesn't have the specific sort of behavior required by that environment? Is the reason because he hasn't developed the appropriate strategy or map to generate that behavior? Is it because he lacks belief, or has a conflicting belief which interferes with his life or his outcome? Finally, is there some interference at the level of identity, of the whole system?

These become very important distinctions for anyone working in the areas of learning, communication or change.

Examples of LOGICAL LEVELS

Logical Levels in a Person

For example, let's say that a child doesn't do well on an exam:

The teacher could say, "It is not your fault at all. Either there was noise in the room or something in the environment that interfered with your performance on the exam."

In other words, the problem is in your environment and has nothing to do with you at all. Of course, this has the least impact on the student.

The teacher could say, focusing on a specific behavior, "You did poorly on this test." That puts the responsibility with the student.

At the capability level the teacher could say, "You are not very good at this kind of material, your capabilities for math or spelling—or whatever it is—are not well developed." This has a wider implication.

On a values level the teacher could say, "Oh well, it is not important. What is important is that you enjoy learning."

The teacher is reinforcing the belief that it is not important to get a good grade, but that enjoying learning is important. Now we have jumped to the level of belief.This goes beyond the subject area to the whole process of learning

On the level of identity, the teacher can say, "You are a poor student," or "You are a learning disabled person" or "You are not a mathematician." This touches the child's whole being.

This level of identity is different from the level of capability. It is different to believe that I am not capable of excelling in a particular subject than to believe that I am a stupid person.

These examples begin to demonstrate the impact of the different levels. There is a very big difference between somebody who says, "I am not capable of controlling my drinking" and somebody who says, "I am an alcoholic and will always be an alcoholic."

If I take something on as part of my identity it begins to have a very profound impact.

Logical Levels in a Company

The same levels will work in organizations and groups as in a person. Here is an example:

Most of you know about computer mouse. I have a question for you: Who invented the mouse?

Most people think the mouse was developed by Apple. The Macintosh is sold by Apple, but Xerox actually paid something like two billion dollars developing STAR, an ancestor of the Macintosh, for Apple even if they didn't realize they were doing it.

What happened there gives you some idea of how these levels work in a company.

In the early 1980s, John Grinder, Richard Bandler and I were doing some consulting for Xerox, and I remember seeing all these computer developments at their research center in Palo Alto. Xerox at this time was in a rather interesting position. (This will also tell you how powerful corporate meta-programs can be. [See Appendix A for a listing of meta program patterns.]) If you think about the identity and meta-program of Xerox, it is: "How do I make a better copy?"

That is making a *match towards past positives*. They make copiers.

They had a problem, though. One of their researchers walked into the *Los Angeles Times* newspaper headquarters and didn't see any paper in the office. Here was a major newspaper and everybody was working with computers and electronic mail.

This started them doing something they were not used to at Xerox. They started looking into the future and started *matching future negatives:* What do you do with a company that makes its living off people copying papers, and ten years in the future there is no paper in offices anymore?

So Xerox started operating away from future negatives and started working on all these developments in personal computers.

The problem is that when you say "Xerox," how many people think of personal computers? They think of photocopies. Xerox was trying to develop these computers but it didn't fit in with their identity; nor did it fit with their corporate belief system, or even with their existing corporate capabilities.

They had research and development capabilities but the rest of their company was not set up to support this development in personal computers.

We told them they were trying to make too big a jump. They were trying to create a whole new identity for themselves, but what happens when you try to do that is conflict; conflict with the old identity and values. And this is exactly what happened at Xerox.

I don't know if you ever heard of their personal computers. They did have one and tried to sell it.

As a matter of fact, what happened was very interesting: it shows you the power of these belief and identity level of meta-programs and how they operate in a company.

I will give you two examples.

1. When they introduced these personal computers to their staff and company, they had somebody dress up as the man who had invented the first Xerox copying machine. He had been dead for fifteen years or so. It seems a bit morbid to have raised him from the dead. They had him introducing this computer as the best, newest version of the Xerox machine: "This is a better reproduction of what I tried to do."

2. The character they used for advertising this computer was a monk! Of course, when you think of high technology a monk is not quite what jumps to mind. What does a monk do? A monk sits down and copies manuscripts. Xerox was so caught up in its meta-program that they did not notice that it didn't match the environment they were trying to enter.

So the predecessor of the Macintosh started off just as an idea in their R and D capability—research and development. At first it was no threat to anybody. It was only a little thing that people were doing at the research center. People who worked there could come in with blue jeans and long hair because, especially in research and development at that time in the history of technology, if somebody didn't have long hair and a beard, no one was really sure he knew what he was doing. If somebody came in with a tie and was clean-shaven they wondered if he was really capable of working with computers.

As they started putting more investment in this new technology and operating away from the future negative, Xerox began to develop the belief they needed it to survive. And they tried to make it part of their identity.

As that happened, there started to be this change over at the research center, where they said, "If this is to become a serious part of Xerox, you will have to fit in with the rest of our identity: shave your beard, cut your hair, wear a tie."

If you think of the meta-programs of researchers, they are mismatchers to the present. They often disdain the way things are in the present in order to match future positives. Also, they want to have their own identity, not only be a small part of this huge identity. They want to be the major part of it.

So when Steve Jobs came over and said he was going to make this technology the heart of Apple's identity, and use it to change the world, what choice do you think these researchers made? The researchers were already in a conflict with the Xerox identity and they were to become only a little part of it, while they could be the corporate symbol of Apple and Macintosh: they jumped right into that.

The point is that even in business you will have different levels and different types of reactions and responses as you make transitions from one level to another.

We actually recommended to Xerox to do what it seems they eventually did. We told them not to jump into personal computers, but to pace and lead their own identity—meaning, start by putting computerized enhancements on their Xerox machines.

If you are worried about not having paper in the future, then develop devices that will scan papers and digitize the words into computers instead of spending your money on making personal computers. Develop technology that will fit more with what you already are.

And that is the sort of thing I believe they have done.

They changed their advertising character to Leonardo da Vinci, who has a different image than a monk and symbolizes more creativity. You have to change your meta-program along with your products.

Logical Levels in Family Systems

The same kind of thing that happened at Xerox will happen as an adolescent grows up in a family. There is a family identity. At first the child is more or less part of the environment. You take care of him, and soon he starts to walk around and develop behaviors. Then you have to start teaching him capabilities: how to guide those behaviors, how to learn not to just randomly break things and move around. Of course, the child develops more and more capabilities through school.

It is only when the child starts developing his own beliefs that you really get in trouble. And when children start developing their own identity, that is when conflict really happens. Very often children want to develop their identity so they won't be just a part of the family. They want to be themselves. They don't want to do things anymore because of what the parents say, or because of what the family wants. They want to do things because they themselves decided to, not because they were told it was best.

This is a rather interesting challenge when you think about it.

"How do you know you are doing something because you really want to do it? How do you know you are not being influenced by what other people have told you, or by the fact that you will get punished if you don't?"

One way is to do something that you know you will get punished for and that nobody wants you to do. Obviously, you will have done it because you are the only one who made the decision. If everybody else is telling you not to do something, and you are going to be in trouble for it, then if you decide to do it, it must have been you. It couldn't be anybody else.

Another way in which people know their identity is by what they can't change. "If I can't change it, it must be part of me, it must be me". In other words, I have got to accept it as being me if I don't know what to do to make it different, and if I can't make it different. What stays the same obviously becomes the most common thread that ties my experiences together.

We will come back to some of the issues of identity later. However, I would like to shift down to the content of the book, which is to deal with beliefs.

The Role of Beliefs

One of the interesting things about beliefs is that because they are on a different level than behavior or capabilities, they don't change according to the same rules.

I will give you an example of a classic story from abnormal psychology of a man who believes he is a corpse. He won't eat, he won't work. He just sits around all the time claiming he is a corpse.

The psychiatrist tries to convince the man that he is not really dead. They have many arguments back and forth. Finally the psychiatrist says, "Do corpses bleed?"

The man thinks about it and says, "No, all body functions have stopped so there is no more bleeding."

So the psychiatrist says, "OK, let's try an experiment. I will take a needle and prick your finger and see if you bleed."

Since the patient is a corpse there is nothing much he can do about it. So the psychiatrist sticks him with the needle and the man starts to bleed. The patient looks at it totally amazed and says, "I'll be damned. Corpses do bleed!"

The point is that when you have a belief, even environmental and behavioral evidence won't change it because a belief isn't about reality. You have a belief in place of knowledge about reality. Beliefs are about things that nobody can know in reality. If somebody has a terminal illness he doesn't know if he is going to get well. There is no present reality as to whether he is going to get well or not. He has to believe that he is going to get well precisely because nobody knows what the reality is.

Another example is the idea of God's existence. There isn't any way of definitely proving it one way or the other. It is a matter of belief or interpretation of certain facts. And, just like the psychiatrist's patient, you can take facts and fit them into belief systems in different ways.

While this story about the patient who thought he was a corpse is humorous, I have known people actually living very similar stories. For example, people who have a terminal illness: AIDS or cancer. Some will actually say that they are dead, they are corpses. What difference does it make what they do? They are going to die. Why should they bother to do anything? They will even take positive evidence and say it is 'just' a remission and they are not really well. They don't want to fool themselves, they will only accept the situation that they are going to die. Arguing with people like that will get you just as far as the psychiatrist did in the story.

There may be a lot of evidence to show that positive attitude and positive beliefs can promote health in serious illness. But how do you get the persons who believe they are corpses to believe that they can be living and healthy? I can tell you that you are not going to do it by arguing with them. I am sure that many of you have tried to change somebody's beliefs by arguing at some point in your lives. You know you can waste a lot of time doing that.

So, beliefs function at a different level than environmental and behavioral reality and don't change by the same processes. In a company, corporate values and policies are changed through a different set of procedures than are used to change machinery.

To better understand the role of beliefs and the processes that influence them, let me review three studies of how beliefs function in the area of behavioral change.

1. Weight Loss

There was an N.L.P. person that I know who decided to research weight-loss programs. In the United States, diet programs are a billion-dollar-a-year industry. The interesting thing about them is that many diet programs are radically different from each other.

Some of them are actually the opposite of each other. Some say, "You can eat anything you want as long as you get exercise." Some say, "It doesn't matter what kind of exercise you get since it is primarily a function of nutrition." Some just work on the particular kind of food you eat. Some have food supplements.

But the amazing thing is that they all work for some people. In other words, they all have effects for some people. So rather than modeling the programs, this person went and asked people for whom different diets had worked, "What happened and how did it work?"

He found there were a couple of common characteristics of these people regardless of which diet program they used.

The first one was that the diet they had chosen accompanied *some other major life change*—maybe a change in their jobs, a change in their relationships, maybe a change in their environment if they had moved somewhere. So it went along with some other life change.

The second thing they all reported was a reaction, which was something like: "This time, *I was really ready to change.*" They were *ready* to lose weight, and I think that quality of readiness is very important, especially in respect to beliefs.

When somebody is ready to change, they can walk into your office and you can blow at them and they will change. You can practically do anything, they are just waiting for permission.

There is a joke that goes, "How many psychoanalysts does it take to change a light bulb?"

It only takes one, but it takes a long time, it is very expensive, and the light bulb has to be ready to change.

So the question now is: *How do you get somebody ready to change?*

If somebody believes that he can change, he will.

2. Recovery From Terminal Cancer

Another interesting survey was done by a person who interviewed one hundred cancer survivors. These were people who had been given a diagnosis of terminal cancer. But ten to twelve years later they were still alive.

This reporter went to interview these different people to try to find out what was the same about them—and as it turned out, the various kinds of treatment they had were very different.

Some had done standard medical treatments, surgery, chemotherapy, radiation. Some had done non-traditional medicine like acupuncture. Some had done diets and nutritional models. Some had followed psychological or religious paths. Some had done nothing at all really.

The only thing that characterized these hundred people was that *they all believed what they were doing would work for them.*

3. Placebos

In medical history there is a very interesting demonstration of the power of belief, which is the *placebo.*

The placebo effect involves a situation where someone who believes he is receiving medication is given a fake drug and actually gets well. It is quite a compelling area to look into.

I first became introduced to it about a dozen years ago when I was doing some research for Grinder and Bandler because they were interested in marketing placebos. They were going to put them in a bottle and call them PLACEBOS. They wanted to compile all the research and just put it in a booklet to go with the bottle.

If you take all the placebo research studies, for instance—and every drug in the United States has to be tested against the placebo—there are volumes and volumes of research on them. And if you look at all this research you will find that on the average a placebo will work as well as a real drug roughly a third of the time—actually more than a third. That is on the average. Some studies show that placebos work as well as morphine *in something like 54% of the cases.*

A man even did a study in the other direction, where he took people who responded to placebos and people who didn't and he gave them real drugs. He gave them drugs for pain such as morphine, and it turned out that the placebo responders responded effectively to morphine over 95% of the time. The other people responded to the morphine 46% of the time. That was roughly a 50% difference, which shows you that even real drugs may require belief to be effective in some cases.

Placebos have even been shown to have an effect in cancer treatment. In fact, in one study they gave people "placebo chemotherapy" and a third of the patients lost all their hair.

The most effective electroshock machine in the state of California was supposedly one that hadn't worked for three years. They gave people a general anaesthetic before they put them on the machine, so mental patients thought they got electroshocks even though they didn't. And that worked better than giving them the actual shock treatment.

So what Grinder and Bandler were going to do was to publish the statistical percentage of placebo effects for various symptoms and the buyer could look down the list of symptoms, look up his chances, and go for it. The label on the bottle would say: *Placebos don't work for everybody, but they might work for you.*

Of course, they were expecting a big uproar from the medical and drug associations. And in the middle of all the controversy they were going to release *Placebo Plus:* twenty percent more inert ingredients in every capsule.

And, in fact, there was some research that showed that a shiny, tiny, red pill that was very expensive had a lot more placebo effect than a fat, chalky, inexpensive one. In other words the sub-modalities of the medicine made a difference.

Later they would release *Mega Placebo*, etc. But I understand Bandler and Grinder were prevented from doing this whole project by the government. Maybe they thought it would ruin the drug industry in the country.

Self-Efficacy-Expectation: The Relationship Between Belief, Capability and Behavior:

The point is that placebos demonstrate the role and the potential power of belief. Beliefs have to do with the future. *The function of belief has to do with the activation of capabilities and behaviors.* Human beings may have a lot of capabilities to influence deep biological processes but we never use them because we don't believe we can.

Until biofeedback came along, nobody could believe that you could even influence your heart rate or your blood pressure. Now we are beginning to believe people can develop those capabilities. Once people begin to believe that they can influence something like cancer, or the immune system, then people will actually begin to engage in the trial and error processes

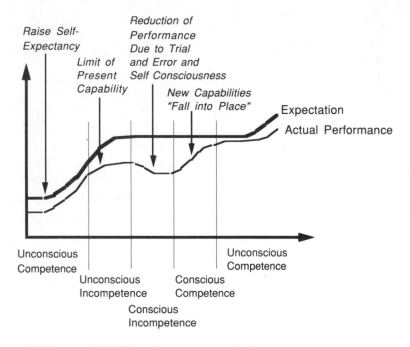

Figure 2. Influence of Self-Efficacy-Expectation on Performance

(or TOTE loops) to develop these capabilities. And it is on this area that I want to focus for a moment.

Albert Bandura of Stanford University has a concept he calls *self-efficacy-expectation,* which is your belief in your own effectiveness in doing something. He takes people who have a fear of snakes and he has them rate their belief about their ability to handle a snake. At first they rate themselves very low and their performance is also very low.

If I don't believe I am going to do very well then my performance is going to stay at about the same level.

Through modeling and counseling he gets people to believe more in their ability to handle snakes. He often finds that the person's belief that he can do it will rise as in the graph shown in figure 2. Generally, the person has some degree of unconscious competence and his performance rises in parallel with the belief, until it reaches a new plateau. At this point the person must maintain the belief or expectation level until the trial and error process required to develop the new capability is complete and the performance improves again.

I find that the same thing happens in health. Somebody believes that he can lose weight but obviously the weight doesn't change just like that—it takes a while. The critical phase is going to be at a specific point of the curve where the belief and the behavior are the most different. The belief levels out and eventually the behavior rises to meet the expectation.

What can happen sometimes is that if a person gets disappointed at this stage, the belief starts to drop. Sometimes it will go even lower than the original competency level. People will revert all the way back. You see this happening when people are trying to lose weight. They will lose weight for a while, reach a plateau, and all of a sudden they will go back and gain even more than they had before.

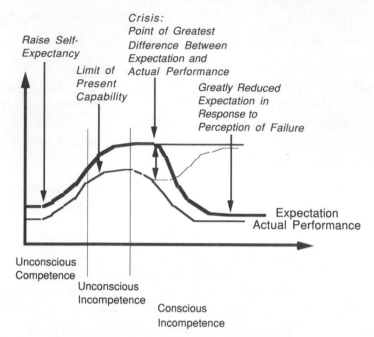

Figure 3. Regression of Expectation Due to Mismatch With Performance

The thing to realize about beliefs is that they are not intended to match existing reality. They are intended to provide a motivation and a vision so that your actual behavior can begin to develop and rise to meet them.

Of course, with the appropriate mental strategy you can improve the performance curve, because you don't have to leave it up to trial and error. If a student believes he can spell or can read but has not been given a strategy to develop the capability, he has to figure out his own strategy for it, and you will see this curve rise more slowly. The slower the curve rises to meet the belief, the more pressure there will be on maintaining the belief.

If I can teach *the strategy for HOW TO,* then the behavior curve rises more quickly and the danger of losing the belief is not as great.

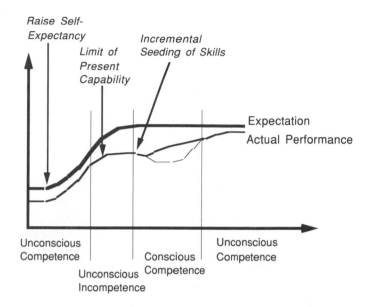

Figure 4. Acceleration of Performance Curve Due to Teaching New Strategies

So you see how capabilities or strategies become important in standing between belief and actual behavior, because the faster I can accelerate the behavior to meet the belief, then the more chance there is that expectations will be met, and the feedback loop continued.

The Role of Environment in Building Beliefs

The environment can also either support or operate against the belief. I will give an example from my own personal history.

About seven years ago my mother had a recurrence of breast cancer, which was a bad sign—recurrence means there has been spreading or metastasis. On top of that, they did a bone scan and found there had been metastasis practically every bone in her body. The doctors elected not to do any radiation or chemotherapy because they didn't think it would make any difference. Basically their attitude was that they would do what they could to "make her comfortable," but she should prepare for the worst.

Instead of losing hope, we began to use various N.L.P. techniques: reframing, building beliefs, visualizations, etc. She began to really learn some things about herself and to develop hope that she could affect her own health. She looked into herself and made some very important discoveries about the transitions she was in at that time. But when she started telling her doctor about what she was doing, the kind of insights she was having, the kind of visualizations, his reaction was, "Don't do that. It is a bunch of poppycock and it will probably just drive you crazy."

When I tried to explain to him some of the potential benefits that had been shown in research on positive attitudes and health, he told me I shouldn't be "experimenting with my mother."

The point is that you have environmental influences, and you have to be able to have a belief that is going to stand up to the pressures from that environment. If the environment is supportive then you have a good support system. But if the environment is not supportive then you will also have to factor that in.

My mother was a nurse and was used to following doctors' orders. So when the doctor in essence writes a prescription for "death" and hands it to you, you are a bit in conflict. When my mother went back to this doctor three months later, he said with a look of surprise, "You look healthier than I do. I guess I have to believe that what you are doing is making a difference. I can't deny it. This is nothing we did."

My mother is now her doctor's "star patient." She still hasn't had any chemotherapy or radiation. But a kind of crisis actually occurred after about eight months or so. Since she was getting healthier the doctor said, "Well, maybe we will do some chemotherapy and radiation just to be sure."

She sort of felt it was like saying, "We will punish you for your success," which was not the intention, but could be felt as being like that.

At another point one of her doctors wanted her to take a particular kind of medication. I was curious to know what the goal was, what they were trying to get to. I was trying to find their *evidence procedure* for successful results. So I asked, "How will we know that she can stop taking it?"

The doctor seemed confused for a moment, and then finally said, "When it stops working, I guess."

This doesn't show great confidence in what one is doing. He didn't realize the *presupposition* behind that statement for the patient; this is the kind of thing that some doctors don't realize.

Eventually they had to gather a group of about fourteen doctors to discuss the case because it was so unusual. They finally decided to let my mother make the decision. And she decided to stay with what she was already doing.

It has been over seven years since the recurrence as of the time of this writing, and she is still very much alive with no symptoms of cancer. She swims half a mile at least four or five times a week. She has traveled to Europe several times and has even been in a couple of television commercials. Sadly, one of the doctors who told her not to build false hopes and prepare herself to die committed suicide not too long ago after finding he had an illness. Perhaps he was a victim of his own self-fulfilling belief system.

The point is that the belief system, the relationship of belief to capabilities and to behavior, and the influence of environment are several issues that we need to address in working with beliefs.

Definition of Beliefs.

Let's now try to define what a belief is a little more precisely. First, a belief is not a strategy; it is not a "how to"; it is not a behavior. *A belief is a generalization about a relationship between experiences.*

1. A belief may be *a generalization about CAUSAL RELATIONS.*

For example:

- What do you believe causes cancer?

- Do you believe that chemicals in the environment cause cancer?

- Is what causes cancer things that you did?

- Things that you think?

- Things that you believe?

- Or is cancer a function of who you are? Your genetic makeup?

Your beliefs will make a difference in how you go about trying to treat cancer.

If you believe it is caused by God as a punishment, it will make a difference in how you try to deal with it.

Beliefs in a company

The same thing is true in a company. I have certainly seen things that would qualify as cancers in a company, or just as severe problems. The question is what you believe to be the cause of those problems.

- Is it the employee? The executive? The lack of training?

- Is it the organizational structure? The organizational culture?

- What is the problem? The business environment? The market place?

What you believe the cause is will determine where you look for the solution. And with the belief you will often find whatever it is that you are looking for. If you believe it is there, you will find it there.

2. A belief may also be a *generalization about MEANING RELATIONSHIPS.*

For example, if I have cancer, regardless of what causes it, what does it mean?

- Does it mean that I am a weak person?

- Does it mean I am just like my mother who died of cancer?

- Does it mean that I hate myself and I am a bad person because I have it?

- Does it mean that I have been putting myself under too much stress?

- Does it mean that I have an opportunity to really learn something?

The meaning you give it will determine how you respond.

If I have a problem in my company: what does that mean?

- Does that mean I am a failure?

- Does it mean I don't deserve to succeed?

- Does it mean I should give up; or try harder?

What does it mean?

3. Finally, beliefs may be generalizations about LIMITS.

I believe that I can affect my health with my beliefs and with my mind up to a point, but above this point I can't.

Where is the limit? How far can I go?

My company can grow up to a certain point but not beyond that.

These three types of generalizations determine the kinds of responses we will have to a particular situation.

Types of Belief Issues

There are typically three types of belief issues that arise from these generalizations. Problems of belief tend to occur around:

- *HOPELESSNESS:* if a person is hopeless he feels or believes an outcome is just not possible. There is no hope.

That is a belief about the outcome. If the outcome is impossible why bother?

For example, nobody gets over AIDS so why bother to try? It is not possible to get well.

- *HELPLESSNESS:* "Some people can get over cancer but they are special people." "I am not good enough, I don't have the capability. It is possible but I am not capable." "Some people have successful businesses, but I don't have what it takes."

- *WORTHLESSNESS:* "It is maybe possible, maybe I have what it takes, but do I deserve it? Have I earned it? Maybe I don't deserve to be healthy. This has to do with my merit." People won't try to get something they don't think they deserve. They will go strongly for something that they do believe they deserve.

WORKING WITH BELIEFS

Now we are going to take a first step in our work on beliefs. We mentioned a little bit about hopeless, helpless, worthless. How do these beliefs get made? How do you have an impact on them? If we are not going to argue what do we do instead? I will tell you one thing, this is a belief I have:

You can only lead people to change their own beliefs. It is not up to you to change somebody else's belief. The goal is to pace and lead them into establishing a new belief for themselves.

Chapter II

BELIEFS ABOUT CAPABILITY

Belief And The Experience of Failure

The place I would like to start working with beliefs is with beliefs about capability and failure. Believing that you are going to fail creates a self-fulfilling prophecy. So if I have tried to lose weight twenty times before and somebody tells me he has a new N.L.P. technique to help me lose weight, I will say, "This is all very good, but it won't work because it never worked before." There were twenty times that are evidence of failure. So I don't really believe it is going to work to begin with. And that belief is important.

A contrast would be people who believe, "If I visualize a success, then I will be able to achieve it."

Somebody told me about some gymnasts. One group was instructed to visualize themselves being able to do a particular move, while the other group was given no instructions. A couple of weeks later, when the time came for them to do this particular move without training, the instructed group had a 50 to 60% success rate, whereas the non-instructed group had only about 10% success.

But what happened to the 40-50% who could not perform even though they visualized? One of the things that I find is that if somebody has a very clear picture of himself being successful but doesn't believe in himself, he says, "I will never be able to do that. **This is just an unrealistic expectation or false hope.**"

"The clearer I see it the more it makes me feel I probably won't be able to do it."

This is an example of how beliefs can affect visualization. Ability to visualize is a function of one's capabilities, but what gives the visualization meaning is the belief.

I know people who are afraid of seeing themselves being successful because then they are sure they won't be able to do it. This illustrates the relationship between belief and strategy. There is more to accomplishing something than knowing how to. In fact, believing that I am going to fail may even make the best technique for success fail. The inverse is also true. Believing in the placebo makes it work.

I once interviewed an inventor who invented this imaging device, which took him many trials to perfect. I asked him how he managed to stick with this goal and go through all those failures. His response was that he didn't think of them as failures, but solutions to problems other than the one he was working on.

How does somebody get to that stage? That is a function of belief. That is not a function of reality. The inventor just believed they were solutions to some other problems, so they became a resource as opposed to a failure.

What I would like to do is to address this issue of failure. The difference between whether something is perceived as feedback or as failure is especially important at the "crisis" point I mentioned earlier, during the discussion of self-efficacy expectation, where a person's expectation about a capability and their actual performance are the most distant from one another.

Turning Failure Into Feedback

I am sure that many of you have goals that you have tried to achieve before without success. And even when you think about them now, you are almost afraid of trying anything new. Why set yourself up for failure again? Why even try some of this new N.L.P. because it will just fail. Even in order to begin to try something you have to be open to it. You have to be ready. How do you get ready? How do you get open?

The following transcript demonstrates how the N.L.P. tools of Accessing Cues, representational systems, and sub-modalities can be used in a combination to make an impact on such a limiting belief.

Demonstration with Linda

R.:   What is your name?

L.:   *Linda.*

R.:   Linda, is there something that you want that you hold yourself back from because of the past?

L.:   *Oh yes.*

R.: As you sit here right now, how do you know that you had a failure? How do you remember that? Just think about what happens when you start feeling badly about it.

L.:   *It happened just now when you spoke about it. I had a feeling here (clutching her stomach) and everything became confused in my head.*

R.:   When you say that you had a feeling and everything became confused, that is a very important statement. I am going to ask you to really think of what it is like. (Linda looks straight down in front of her.) That is good enough for the moment.

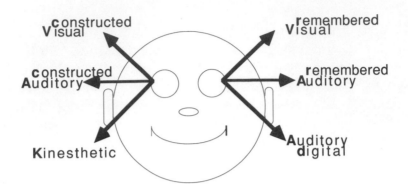

Figure 5. Standard NLP Accessing Cue Chart

(To the audience): I have a question for you. What accessing cue was that? Was it kinesthetic? Where was it exactly? Was it down to the right? Was it down to the left? It was down in the middle. What accessing cue is that?

R.: (To Linda again): Let me ask a few questions. When you go into that do you see any pictures?

L.: *When I enter into it, no. When I begin to think, yes.*

R.: Do you hear voices?

L.: *No... Maybe... yes.*

R.: No? Maybe? Yes? Well, I can see why you are confused!

My guess is that if you start exploring it, you will find that every representational system is in there.

But as she says, when she gets into it there is no specific representational system. It is mostly kinesthetic. I find this very interesting. This is what you call a synesthesia in

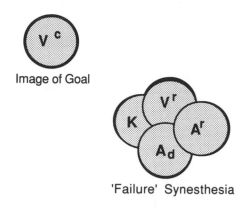

Image of Goal

'Failure' Synesthesia

Figure 6. Synesthesia: "Molecule" of Sensory Experiences

N.L.P. A strategy is a sequence of representational systems but in a synesthesia they all get grouped together. And they will feed off each other.

Linda, what is your goal? I don't want you to tell me. I just want you to think about it. Do you have an image of it? Words? Feelings?

L.:   *I have a representation.* (Looks up and right.)

R.:   Let me give a metaphor. In organic chemistry, various elements combine to make molecules, and it doesn't take too much thinking to see that part of what is happening with Linda is kinesthetic and auditory and visual remembered—all combined together here, down in front of her, to make a molecule for failure. And floating above the molecule you have a single visual construct of some desired goal.

(To the audience): I ask you, if she tries to do this behavior, which one do you think will win out? The molecule is all connected together, it is much more powerful. Look at the physiological aspect when I ask her to think about her goal. She said,

"I have A representation."

But the failure experience is a synesthesia of many representations and she is drawn right into it. We are going to use accessing cues here because I think each one of these representations is important and fine, but just not in the way they are being put together. In other words, "Why did God make accessing cues?" God made accessing cues so we could sort things out; so you can distinguish your feelings from your pictures and so on. But Linda's failure experience is not auditory or visual or kinesthetic, and her eyes are not in any standard N.L.P. eye position. They were straight down in front of her. She said, it is 'confusion'. Obviously, at the conscious level that confusion is going to be more kinesthetic and auditory, with a large lack of clarity because the eye position is down.

(To Linda): So, we are going to sort these representations to their proper accessing cues. I would like you to go into this state and just take the feelings, and put your eyes down to the right and then take the sounds and put them down to the left. So first start here, and it is OK to have that feeling.

I would like you to actually take the feeling and put your eyes down to the right, just with those feelings. That's right.

Then come back to the middle and take any sounds or words that you hear. Can you hear them? You can hear them over here. Move your eyes down here to the left.

Then go back to the middle and take any pictures that are there, but bring them up here to your left where you can

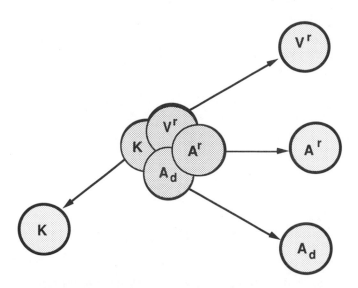

Figure 7. Seperating and Sorting the Synesthesia "Molecule"

visualize them. Put them into visual memory. Now go back to this failure place, and anything that comes up, sort it to where it belongs. Make the feelings go to the right, words to the left, the images up and left. OK, good. Now let's go to the feelings that you put down and to your right.

When you go to those feelings just by themselves, with no pictures, no words, no sounds, just you and your feelings, what happens? How does that feel?

L.:   *The feelings are not so important anymore.*

R.:   Notice when a feeling is just a feeling, it is not a belief, it is a feeling. Is it failure? What would you call that feeling? What is that feeling?

L.:   *It is just somehow annoying.*

R.:   OK, this is just annoying. I have a question: How do you know that feeling is annoying?

L.:   *Because I don't feel well inside.*

R.:   One comment: **If you have a bad feeling, how do you know it is 'bad?'**

(To the audience): What some people call fear some other people call excitement. I was doing this process with a person who had a feeling she had always called despair. Then she began to be with it and examine it. It turned out that what this feeling was really about was being on the verge of discovery. It wasn't really despair; it was actually being ready to make a big leap. The reaction to it was based upon how she compared it to the other representations in the molecule.

L.:   *When you asked me if there was a connection with fear...when I have a big fear I also have the same impression.*

R.:   So I would like you to go back to that feeling by itself, and first **find out what the feeling is communicating.** If it is just a feeling, can you move it a little bit? If you took that same feeling and you moved it up or spread it out a little bit, would it be the same? What happens?

L.:   *It is lighter.*

R.:   (To the audience): Here is another interesting thing. If I take the feeling as a feeling then I can begin to get it to work for me. It is not this confusion anymore. It is a feeling that I can actually begin to use in my service. (To Linda): What would you like that feeling to do?

L.:   *I would like it to be excitement.*

R.:   What would you need to do for that? What would happen to it if it became excitement? Would it become lighter?

Would it move more?

L.: *It would become more dynamic.*

R.: How would you do it? Would you move it more? Can you shift it slightly so it can become more dynamic?

L.: (Moment of silence.)

R.: Alright, I am going to leave that for just a moment. (To the audience): What we have done is take the feeling by itself, and pace and lead it.

It is not a 'bad' feeling, it is just a feeling. What is its communication? What could it do to work more for you? (To Linda): Let's come here to the words. Are there specific words? Are there a lot of them or a few of them?

L.: *It is an internal dialog.*

R.: Is it your voice? Nobody else, just you?

L.: *There are other voices but it is my voice first.*

R.: What does this voice say?

L.: *It is criticizing.*

R.: So just listen to the voice. No feeling, no pictures; so you can hear it criticizing, but it is just a voice. What is the intention of this voice?

L.: *As a voice only? Well, if it is only as a voice, there is no bad intention.*

R.: Why is it saying these things then? Habit? Something you have learned from your parents?

L.: *It probably is habit.*

R.: What should be the intention of this voice then? What was it developed for?

And if it is just habit it is something that you have said before and it doesn't belong to your internal dialog. It belongs to memory.

(To the audience): This is another thing: Your parents' voices don't belong in your internal dialog; they belong to memory. So let's take the old habit and put it in the auditory memory eye position straight to the left, since that seems to be where it belongs.

(To Linda): Can you do that? Can you move it up here and hear it with your eyes over there to the left? Now that you put that habit over here, what is down in your inner dialog?

L.: *If the voice is here, I can switch it off.*

R.: What would you say to yourself now, down here, in your internal dialog? What kind of voice would you use?

L.: *I would have choice between many voices.*

R.: Now we have a choice. I am going to leave that for the moment as it is. Again, we pace, acknowledge, and lead the voice.

Let's go up to those memories. They are just images of memories.

In fact, people will often develop these failure synesthesias for the purpose of knowing 'reality.' They want to remember the "truth," but if I took all my bad pictures and my nasty voices and my bad feelings and stuck them all together, would that be reality? Would that be the truth?

I mean, if you look at those pictures up there, they are not the only pictures in your life. They are not even the only memories that may relate to your outcome or goal. Often if you look at these memories all in relationship to themselves that relationship spells out "FAILURE"; but if you look at these memories in relationship to your goals, you may begin to recognize that in those pictures there actually are some partial successes.

Now when you look at the pictures in relationship to other successes in your life they don't spell out "FAILURE" anymore. They might even be very different. They are learnings.

(To Linda): I would like you to go back and forth between those memories and the representation of your goal. In fact, I want to make sure that when you look to the right you can visualize your goal, that you do see what you want. Clarify this representation and then go back and forth between these memories, on your left, and that goal on your right, and see what you can learn from those pictures. For example:

Are these memories actually taking you away from that goal?

Or are they actually leading right in the direction of that goal?

They could be a progression towards that goal. (To audience): As she does that I want to reiterate the point that if I look at my mistakes in relation to each other, they look like failure.

If I look at my mistakes in relation to my goal or my other successes they are "FEEDBACK." And this is the interesting thing about beliefs; they are about relationships and meaning. Those memories are what they are. That is the content. What you learn from them is based on how you compare them and what you are looking for.

R.:   My next question is:

Can you see a relationship between all this?

L.:   *In some sense yes, because over here (points up left) I took out all the feelings and took what was interesting about success over there, (points up right) but now the goal is not the same.*

R.:   Notice that the feedback has even updated the goal. Is that goal just as valuable to you?

L.:   *This goal is more valuable.*

R.:   What you are saying is, rather than having this sort of dream, this hope, just floating around up here, when you take the pieces that you learn from the memories, it actually changes this goal to something different from what you were going for when you had these so-called "failures."

L.:   *The goal is still basically the same, but I took from the pictures only positive parts of my life and erased negative parts.*

R.:   There is another good strategy for doing that: these memories make the resourceful parts literally brighter, so when you look back over your experiences they stand out, while the other ones sort of fade in between. It is the same content; you are not trying to ignore or hide anything—it is rather what you choose to pay attention to in terms of your outcome. Both contents are just as real.

The question is to choose if the cup is "half empty" or "half full."

Now, these memories that were put down here in a garbage can, as if they were really disgusting, we will actually find that within them there are pearls, jewels. Why were they put in this "failure" garbage can? You can use them now as a resource. You can find the jewels in them shining from your history.

And now to the last step: We have the former failure feelings down and right and a choice of voices down and left. We have memories of what you used to say that you can either turn up or down.

There is an interesting thing you can even do with these memories if they are critical voices that say things like: "You can't do that" (negative tone).

You can even keep the same content and change the meta-message given by the voice tone: "You can't do that?" (disbelief).

It is the same verbal message but what matters is the meta-message.

You can keep exactly the same verbal content but change the tone of voice, and by altering the voice tone, by making it questioning and mocking, like in a challenge; then the meta-message is: "You are really sure that you can't do this, that you are not able to do this?"

The change of tone enables you to change the meaning and turn it into a challenge. Of course, the same words are used, but by changing the sub-modalities of the tone, the impact is totally different. Remember when you use sub-modalities to shift the meta-message you can change the meaning of the same content as you want.

What we want to do now is bring these elements back together into a new molecule. What we did was to put these visual memories up here, on the left. The auditory went here, in the middle, and the kinesthetic point was down there, on the right. You might even want to mix some new auditory from the auditory construct position, straight and to the right, to support you.

In other words, if you took this goal that you have, can you hear what your voice would sound like as you are achieving it? Where would you speak from? What kind of resonance would it have? And put all that right over there to the right.

Now we want to bring all these representational systems back together, but in such a way that they support each other in going towards the goal. The feelings support these words and these pictures and these memories, and these memories support these goals and these words and these feelings. Create a synesthesia in which, instead of tearing each other apart, the more images you have the stronger the feeling and the louder the voice of support, and the more voice the brighter the memories.

Now we have something that is more like a genetic structure. We have a kind of double helix that supports itself and reproduces itself in a system of harmony and beauty rather than a mess, a confusing soup of feelings. And the important thing is that we don't want to ignore or disqualify any of that content, any of those original pieces that were there. It is a matter of restructuring the harmony of the system.

There is an easy way of doing this, using N.L.P. strategy technology. We will map over to a positive reference. The basic process is to find a reference experience with some other content that fits the kind of resourceful structure we want to put together here.

R.: (To Linda): Can you think of something else that you know you will do in the future but that you haven't done yet? There may be all kinds of problems, but you are sure that you are going to be able to do it.

(Linda looks straight ahead with eyes slightly raised.)

(To the audience): Now look at the accessing cue. It is very common, but we don't find it in the accessing cues that are usually taught. It is not visual remembered up to the left, visual construct up to the right, auditory right in the middle. **It is straight ahead and up by about 15 or 20 degrees.**

R: (To Linda): And do you have feelings and pictures and sounds?

L.: *Of course.*

R.: That is another synesthesia accessing cue. We can now take the images, sounds and feelings formerly associated with failure and organize them into this existing resourceful synesthesia structure. First we will do the visual part. We want to make these images match the structure of how you know you can do something. Take the image of your goal and put it out there straight in front of you and a little up. And make sure it is the same distance, the same brightness, the same size, the same quality of movement, the degree of color, the same depth and vividness as the resource experience. Where do the memories go in your positive reference experience? Do they go behind you, do they just stay up to the left?

L.: *They are probably behind.*

R.: Rearrange these memories that were formerly associated with failure to go behind you so they can support the future goal. Now what about sounds, voice? In the reference experience that you already know you can do, what do you hear? Where? How?

L.: *I can hear inside but the voice is not the same. The voice agrees with the acting.*

R.: Can you take the voices that we put down left and bring them inside? Can they support you going towards the goal? You said you were not even sure that you would need a voice. But if you bring them back in, do they support that action? What about the old voice? Where does that belong, what kind of quality would it have?

L.: *The old one is over there and I can switch it off.*

R.: How about the sounds of the outcome in the positive reference example? Are sounds associated with it? Do they come from the front, from inside, from behind?

L.: *They are other voices and especially one. The sound is clear. Everything is calm. Inside voices are supporting the acting.*

R.: **Last step: the feelings.** Do you remember those feelings of annoyance? Bring those into the new synesthesia and find out what they do. Do they transform, do they become lighter? How do they fit in relation to the goal? Because you need those feelings.

L.: *I told you about some fear, feeling of fear. It still exists somewhere but it is supporting now.*

R.: That is an interesting thing about fear; it can be disguised motivation. People often call fear having "butterflies in your stomach"; and the question is not how to kill the butterflies, but rather to teach them to fly in formation. They can tell you something is important, and be there as a motivation.

My final question: Do you believe that you can accomplish that goal now?

L.: *Probably.*

R.: Probably? Probably isn't good enough. Let's do some fine tuning. What is the difference between that other goal you are sure you can achieve, and this one you now believe you can probably do?

L.: *Well, I am not sure about this one, but I am sure about that one. (Linda lowers her eyes back to the initial position of the first belief.)*

R.: Don't look down there. Bring that goal up here. It goes here now. It is not down there anymore. Look up, up here and put it completely there.

L.: *I try to put it up over there but I am not sure it is really over there.*

R.: Aha! How would you know it is really there? When I ask you if you can reach this new goal now, how is it different from your resourceful reference experience?

L.: *The resource is connected to a positive experience in the past.*

R.: And this one is not connected? To which positive experience do you need to connect it?

(To the audience): By the way, she is telling you something very important about how she builds a belief. After we make the representation clear and we get all the senses supporting it, we then have to connect it to other experiences that are positive. (To Linda): Can you do that?

L.: *Yes I can.*

R.: Are you sure?

L.: *Yes. I can connect it to something positive that I did before, a project, and put them together.*

R.: This is an important part of how people build a belief: she is making more of a molecule. (To Linda): And now are you sure you can reach your goal?

L.:   *Of course! No problem.*

R.:   I believe you. Now, since it is lunchtime I would like to leave all this as food for thought, and as you digest everything that we have been doing, you might find there are even other things you could connect that goal with. And you can allow your subconscious to surprise and delight you with just how many connections you might be able to make once you start.

Thank you.

Exercise

The first thing to remember is that a belief is most likely going to involve some kind of combination or synesthesia of senses. It is going to combine different representational systems. Our goal is (1) to find out what this molecule of senses has been, (2) to separate and sort those parts out, and then (3) to reorganize them into a new relationship.

Part One

Step one: The specific steps of the process involve first *identifying the problem attitude or belief.* This normally comes up at those 'crisis' times where your expectations and performance are most apart from one another.

For example, what is something that you want to do, but you hold yourself back from because of past failure or concern? Find the state you go into, the belief, and find the physiology and eye position associated with that belief. It might be something that you want to try, but get the feeling you just can't, or you want to do, but you are afraid that you might fail or that something will happen.

Once we identify where the eye position is, where this belief happens, where the limiting belief comes up, then you will probably find out that this position is going to have all the senses involved in it, and you are going to be seeing and hearing all feelings all at once. And, as in Linda's case, it will probably be all confused together.

Step two: Our second step is to *separate out the synesthesias by putting each of these sensory representations into the appropriate N.L.P. eye accessing position*—so the visual memory goes up and left, and the internal words go down and left, and feelings down and right. There might also be constructed images that you can put up and right to sort them where they go.

Then you address each of these representations individually. *What is the purpose of this feeling?* How do I know it is negative? Maybe it is not. So I want to acknowledge each of these representations, pace them and then lead them a little bit. Once the feeling is just a feeling, I can change it to something a little different. The same will happen with the internal voice. What is its intention? How would I change it a little bit to make it fit that intention better?

There is one point that I should bring up. *If somebody has difficulty separating them out*—if the person can't separate the pictures from the feelings, for instance—*then you can use submodalities.*

You might have the subject put the pictures in a frame, move it far away, and then move it up and left.

If they say that the voice and the feelings don't separate, take the voice and turn it to a whisper, and then move it. You may need a little bit of creativity at that stage. That will be up to you. It is something that you can't predict. It will be a function of your ability to use feedback.

Also remember that as you work with a person, get right next to them. And if you have this molecule, this belief right here, make it real and concrete. Reach out and grab those pieces and separate them. Take the pictures and literally lead the person to relocate them by physically pushing them up.

Your activity and your physical involvement will help to make that separation easier.

Step three: After you have the communication of each part, then you *take the visual memories,* and find out: *Is there something new that you can learn from these memories?*

And remember, that means *looking at the memories in relationship to other memories of successes, and in relationship to the outcome, the goal.*

I will give you an example.

Here is a past experience; if I just look at it by itself, it only means one thing, but if I look at what it tells me in relationship to my outcome, I learn something different from it. The information is not in the picture itself. It is in how the picture relates to where I want to go. The idea here is to begin to see that *these experiences are not failures, they are feedback.*

I can take parts that were successful and focus on those to help me get here.

Step four: At this point, I want to be able to *see a connection to the goal and maybe modify the goal,* add to it, change it a little bit based on what I have learned from these memories.

I have had this goal that I set maybe a long time ago. This goal might change a little bit. It might become updated based on what I learned. I might have set a goal for something, three years ago, that I would update somehow now. I know more, I have learned more. So this goal actually becomes richer, and more related to who I am now.

Some people still have childhood fantasies that they are try-ing to achieve that are not realistic for who they are anymore. So those can be made more adult-like, more realistic in the context of what you have learned from personal history.

So, to backtrack to Part One of the exercise: We put all those pieces of the limiting synesthesia out to their appropriate accessing positions, examine each of them individually—what the intention is—and lead it a little bit.

A bad feeling might not be a bad feeling if you adjust it a little bit. Maybe it becomes lighter or more exciting—to make it fit its intention a little bit more. If it is a voice, for instance, maybe I will change the tone of the voice a little bit, or get it more distant.

So we organize the parts of the synesthesia out to the periph-ery, then we start to learn from these past experiences so they become feedback instead of failure. This is the first half.

Part Two

In the second half, we want to *take all these pieces and put them back together.*

And that is where the positive reference experiences come in. I want to take all these pieces that I have sorted out and put them back together in the same structure as a goal that I am confident I can achieve.

This involves two steps.

Step one: *I find a reference experience* for something, with a different content from the desired goal associated with the fail-ure belief, that I already know I can get to. Let me put in a little content so it becomes clear—because while this can be done without knowing the content, I think it will help you to have some content just to sort them out.

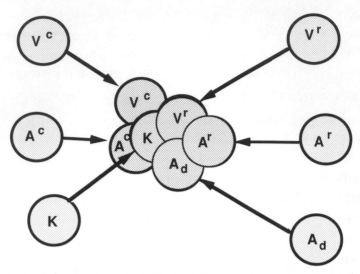

Figure 8. Creating a New Synesthesia "Molecule"

Let's say that your goal is to be a thin person; You want to lose weight. That is the content of what you had the failure feelings about, and we've separated it all out to these pieces.

Now I ask: *What is some other goal that you are already sure that you will be able to get to in the future?*

The reason I want to pick something from the future is that you haven't accomplished this goal yet, but there are things that you know you are going to get to in the future, things that you have confidence and have belief about. We want to give that same feeling to the desired goal of becoming thin.

Q: *Is it necessarily something that we have already done?*

A: No, not necessarily. You just want it to be something that you know that you are going to be able to do. It is a belief about a capability.

Here is an example: I know that I am going to be taking a vacation. I planned this vacation. It is coming up in two weeks, and there might be problems at work, and the plane might be late, but I am going to take that vacation. I will get there somehow.

Or it might be a seminar that I planned. There could be a lot of problems happening, but I will figure a way around them to put that seminar on. It could be buying a house. I know there are going to be a lot of things getting in the way but it is something that I am sure that I can get eventually.

The point is that **it is not so much a belief that the goal will happen as it is a belief about your capability to make goals happen.**

We never know reality in the future. And that is not the point. The point is to organize this representation of your desired goal in the same way as you represent goals that you believe you can accomplish. What we are after is something that hasn't happened, but that you have the capability to confidently work towards.

You have a relative certainty that you can handle all the problems that could come up. You believe in yourself and that you can get there; a positive self-efficacy expectation.

That is the kind of reference you want. So I might be sure that I am going to organize a party, or that I am going to finish some paper or article that I have been working on. I know it is something that I am going to finish eventually, and anything that gets in the way is just feedback.

Let's say, I have confidence that I can buy a new house. Now, what I want to do is take all these things about losing weight, and make them fit the same structure as the way I think about buying a house.

On one side, there is the way I am thinking about losing weight; on the other side, there is the way I am thinking about buying a new house.

Step two: I want to *make all the sub-modalities of losing weight match the sub-modalities* of buying a new house.

That means that if when I think of buying a new house the picture is in front of me, and when I think of losing weight the picture is up to the right, I want to move the picture of losing weight from up right to be in front of me.

Notice that we're *not substituting one content* (losing weight) *for another* (buying a new house).

The content is not important. This is: *I want to represent them both with the same structure, so I have equal confidence with both.*

Now I go down the list of possible sub-modality differences. Is the location of the sound when I think of buying a new house coming from within, or from the outside? What I want to do is move the voices and the sounds when I think of losing weight to the same place.

So I am utilizing a belief strategy. You build up your mental map of this goal so that it has the same richness and robustness of the map of something else that you are sure you can get to. That's it.

Q.:   *Do the level of the reference and the goal in the experience have to be the same level for the person? For example, I am almost certain that I am going to have a cup of coffee tomorrow, but it doesn't necessarily have the same importance as my goal.*

R.:   That is a good question. I think that the closer they match in the kind of feeling and in the kind of meaning, the better it is. I think that the more it really involves your commitment, the more convincing it will be to you.

A comment about this exercise:

This is a process about feedback. People can always creatively come up with things that you don't expect. I invite you to consider these opportunities and challenges for feedback rather than saying, "I failed and something is going wrong."

Remember that there are other types of belief issues than beliefs about capabilities. You may very well discover what those issues are during this exercise. This is not a panacea. This is not a cure. It may not completely resolve all problems. It is just a beginning.

It is like learning to be a magician. It is one thing to make a card disappear, but it takes a little more to make an elephant disappear. We are going to start with cards here, and by the time you finish the course, you will be conjuring elephants, maybe even hippopotami!

Q.: *In which situation do you anchor and when?*

R.: When the person thinks of the positive reference and I see him enter that state of certainty, I anchor that. And then when I am putting my goal into its new place, in order to help that new molecule come together, this anchor becomes the glue to secure it.

Realize that you are really doing two things with this process: *You are using the person's resource strategy, and you are doing this reorganization of the molecule.*

And I expect it to be somewhat challenging to some of you. But I have a great certainty that you will be able to complete this in a way that allows you to learn something new, and begin to bring these processes together so you are using, at the same time, a number of different skills.

Q.: *Was there only one anchor? From here, we had the feeling there were several anchors.*

R.: I am always using anchors. When Linda first thought of the negative experience, I anchored it to help me get back to it.

You could collapse those at the end if you want. I use these so unconsciously that if I am standing next to somebody at a coffee break and he has a good feeling, I anchor myself.

But again I would like you to develop a flexible idea about all these things. Use whatever helps you.

You might use sub-modalities inside this exercise in certain places. Think about it this way: *This technique, or any technique, is a skeleton.*

The thing that puts flesh on the skeleton and life into it, is you. There are things that you may be able to do simply because of who you are, and because of the eye contact you have with that person, and they will be worth more than any step in a technique.

It is your identity that is going to make this work. Don't ever be afraid to drop in your intuitions to make something work. That is my invitation to you.

Q.: *I don't understand why the connection between the memories and the goal is necessary.*

R.: Because if these memories have nothing to do with the outcome, there is no continuity, no support. People may say, "Oh here is my outcome, but it doesn't fit with anything that I have done in my life."

Then they are going to run into a conflict.

We want to be able to see that these things fit together. If you have an outcome that doesn't fit with anything about you, then you are going to have to address that.

Q.: *What does that mean in terms of sub-modalities?*

R.: You will actually sense the connection in some way, even if you just see a color, or a line that connects the experiences together, or even if you just have the feeling that they fit together. The important part is that it forms a gestalt, that my outcome fits in with my experience. If you can get that sense that is enough.

It is best to initially practice this in groups of three. Find out what happens in yourself as you go through this process. Switch roles when you finish each person.

The following is a brief summary of the entire process:

Failure into Feedback Strategy

1. Identify the problematic attitude or belief.

   a. Observe the physiology and eye position associated with the belief.

   b. Find out what is happening internally in each of the representational systems (VAK) during the belief.

2. Separate the **VAK** *"synesthesia"* by putting each sensory representation into the "appropriate" N.L.P. eye position.

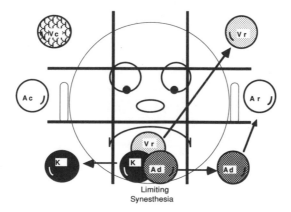

Figure 9. Sorting the Limiting Synesthesia

3. Look up and right *(to visual construction)* and visualize the desired goal/attitude/belief.

    a. Check the *communication* (positive intent) of the feeling (by itself) and the words (by themselves) *in relationship to the desired goal* as opposed to the past memories.

4. Look at the pictures of the memories associated with the belief and build a more realistic perspective on the total situation by intermixing positive memories with the memories associated with the problem, so that they fit on your time line in the appropriate time sequence.

    a. See how the formerly negative memories can actually provide positive feedback that can lead you directly to the desired goal.

    b. You may even want to modify or add to the desired goal based on what you learned from looking at the memories.

    c. Make sure you can see steps that can connect the memories and the positive goal.

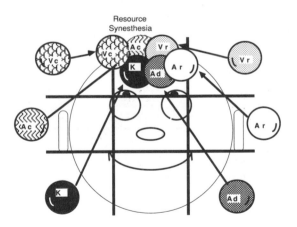

Figure 10. Creating a Resource 'Molecule'

5. Identify a positive, resourceful reference experience; i.e., something you are sure you can achieve in the future.

   a. Establish an anchor for the experience.

6. Make the **VAK** sub-modality qualities of the desired goal the same as those of the positive reference experience.

   a. Fire the anchor for the positive reference while looking at the desired goal to help this process.

Questions Following the Exercise

I would like to find out now what kinds of questions, reports, comments came from doing this exercise with each other.

Q.: *My client was very auditory, and if I had listened to myself—being rather visual—I would have made her work on the visual mode. But visualizing and all visualization were much more difficult for her. We did fight our way to it auditorily, but it took longer. I hesitated between my desire to follow her or to follow you.*

R.: What do you think I would have recommended? If you asked, what would I say? I would say, follow her. Following me is following her. *N.L.P. was made to help clients*, not to make clients fit N.L.P. I would like to congratulate you for recognizing it. Noticing that about your client was very important.

   I think you should congratulate yourself as well.

In terms of setting outcomes or goals, visual is not the only system. I tend to start with vision because it is easier to proceed to the gestalt with vision, but it is certainly not the only way. You can hear a voice that includes within it all voices, and you probably even recognize that there are times that you speak with a voice that speaks with all voices. You can also hear within it a deeper resonance of all of you.

I think there is another issue, which has to do with how clear the vision should be anyway—or the representation of the outcome if it is not visual. When people set goals and outcomes, it is typically in terms of behaviors.

So if you want to make a picture of it, you make a picture of behaviors.

But how do you represent an outcome on the identity level? I may find it is not a behavioral "goal".

Identity is not based on a specific goal or any particular outcome.

At the level of identity you have what might be called a mission rather than a specific outcome.

And very often a person who is working with an identity issue won't be able to identify a specific goal because it is irrelevant.

A mission could incorporate many, many goals. And related to your particular issue, *there may not be a specific picture. It is more a direction.*

And that is a much more powerful level at which to operate anyway.

Sometimes people in a company start arguing about goals and don't realize that is not what the issue is. If the organization doesn't have a mission it's easy to argue about goals. *Goals rise from the mission.*

Mission is a very different level of process. It is more about values and criteria than about some practical and specific results.

And if the specific goal conflicts with the mission, guess what is going to be thrown out?

Q.: *When you say "mission," is it possible to be aware of it if you don't believe in God, for instance?*

(Some laughter in the audience.)

R.: That is a good question.

I don't know. It depends on what you mean by God. It is an interesting point and I would like to address it.

I change or operate on my environment, through my behavior. *To change my behavior, I have to be at the level up above it: capabilities.*

I can't really understand or change my behavior until I am above it.

This capability level is like the puppeteer who is working a marionette.

To change a capability I am going to have to be at the level above that: the level of belief.

And to change a belief, to get outside of my beliefs so I can really look at them and change them, I will begin to operate from pure identity.

So the question is: If I start to question, to change my identity, my mission, and I have to be at the level above, what level is that?

That is not identity, that is not about me. It is not about my ego, it is broader than my mission, it is about being a member of a much vaster system. And I think that is a spiritual level.

That is why I say it depends on what you mean by God.

I think at the point where you are trying to determine your mission, or you are unsure of who you really are anymore, you have to address issues on this "spiritual" level. I don't think it necessarily has to fit into any existing religious dogma, but it operates at a very deep level. It is a question that one has to answer for oneself to resolve this issue of mission.

I don't think there is any way for a person who has a terminal illness to be able to make the changes that he needs until he is able to jump to that level to find his life's meaning, the will to live. In fact, I think it is an interesting coincidence that the term we use to describe a person's recovery from a life-threatening illness is "re-mission."

And beyond that, outside of illness, I think that people who make up the geniuses of history are the ones who for whatever reason do get up to this spiritual level in their own work. Their

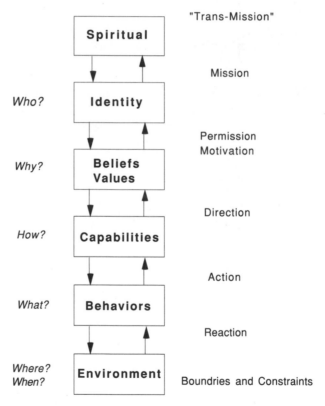

Figure 11. Questions and Goals at Different Logical Levels of Systems.

work isn't about themselves. Mozart said that his work didn't come from him. And regardless of how you think about it, what he was saying is that his music wasn't a function of his ego or identity. His harmony was an expression of something outside his particular identity or belief. Mozart said, "I am constantly searching for two notes who love each other."

If identity involves mission, I think spirituality involves something like "trans-mission" (in both senses of the term i.e. that which is transmitted and received, and that which crosses many missions.).

The same is true with somebody like Albert Einstein. In fact, about his work in the field of physics, Einstein said, "I am not interested in this spectrum of light, or how much this molecule weighs, or what this particular atomic structure is. *I want to know God's thoughts. Everything else is details.*"

I don't think this was an egotistical statement. That was a statement of what his mission was. He didn't say, "I want to become famous by changing physics," or "I am going to show these jerks what I think is right."

He said, "God shows himself in a harmony of everything that exists." And physics was his search for God.

God was in the patterns and relationships between the things that happened in the universe.

So I think it is very important when you say, "How can you answer questions concerning mission without addressing the issue of God in some way?"

I agree with you, it is not a laughing matter.

I think that this totality of levels is important. Some people are able to affect the world through their behaviors. Other people affect the world through their influence on peoples' beliefs.

Some people can affect the world purely through their identity, by who they were as a figurehead. The ones who really stand out are the ones who don't only affect the environment and our day-to-day behaviors and our capabilities or knowledge or thinking and our beliefs and identities, *but also our spiritual levels.* The more levels something affects, the more complete the impact is.

When we are working to change a person, organization, or family, sometimes the problem is behavior, sometimes the problem is belief, and sometimes the problem crosses a number of these levels.

I have seen people getting into this attitude with N.L.P. where they only want to do magic. The attitude is that "If it takes you more than twenty minutes, you must have done it wrong."

But I can tell you that when I was working with my mother to assist her in her recovery from cancer, I wasn't using quick, slick tricks, and I don't want to use tricks when I work with anybody else.

The question is: *How do I bring all of these levels into the work I am doing?*

In fact, I think that during this exercise, some of you probably found that even though you started with a belief about capability, *you ended up on a deeper level.*

When you break up the molecule surrounding the failure feeling, when you peel those layers away, you find it is not just a belief about capability. You suddenly find that maybe it goes to a belief about yourself.

> *It is not so much that I don't believe I am capable of this; maybe I believe that I don't belong here.*

> *Maybe it is at a core level that I believe I am a fake.*

> *And that becomes a very important discovery.*

If that happened in this exercise, if you got through this first belief just to find something that seemed deeper—that is not a failure, that is a success. I don't necessarily think that this technique is designed to deal with identity issues. This leads us, however, to our next question: *How do we deal with beliefs about identity?*

And this is one of the issues that we want to begin to address with other skills and other techniques.

One of the things I have done for years is to try to use the tools that I have (N.L.P. and other tools) to study the strategies of effective people. One of the persons I have been studying recently is Jesus.

Alignment of All Levels

I studied the verbal patterns Jesus used and what I could learn about his belief system and strategies. I found it very interesting to go through his Commandments.

When Jesus was challenged to answer what the greatest Commandment was, he jumped to a higher logical level. He didn't say, "Thou shalt not do this or that behavior."

No outcomes stated in the negative.

He said that the first and most important Commandment was "Love your God with your heart, your mind, your soul, and your strength."

When we think of what it means in relationship to the levels we've been exploring, it is saying to organize yourself towards

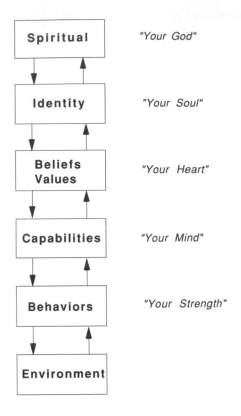

Figure 12. Alignment of Logical Levels

your highest spiritual purpose (God), with your heart (your beliefs), your mind (your capabilities), your soul (your identity), your strength (your behavior). *Basically there was an alignment of all those levels.*

Jesus also said there was a second Commandment as important as the first, but it comes after the first: *To love your neighbor as yourself.*

Once you are aligned and congruent, then love people around you as you would yourself. In N.L.P. language, this would mean the ability to take "second position." That is to be able to put yourself into another's model of the world and value it as your own.

But notice that if I am not aligned at all these levels, if I have a conflict and I hate myself, then I am incongruent, and *I am sure I will treat my neighbor just like I treat myself, with hatred and incongruity.*

This comes first: congruency inside.

But if I only have personal congruency and am not able to understand and respect another person's model of the world I can bowl other people over and not even notice.

This is what happened in the Crusades. Everybody was going for God with their heart and soul and mind and strength... and killing their neighbors. That is missing the second Commandment.

That is one of the interesting things about personal power. I really do believe that both of those things are needed for balance, and that they come in that order. Hopefully that is how you all will be by the time you complete this course—or at least closer.

The Example of Milton Erickson

When Milton Erickson was 19 years old he was struck down by polio. He couldn't move, he couldn't talk. Everybody thought that he was in a coma. And there he was, 19 years old on the threshold of his life, trapped inside a body that didn't respond in any way.

Somebody could feel angry about that. You could perceive that as a confirmation that you were not worthwhile. You could feel helpless. Erickson could certainly have felt hopeless, especially when he heard the doctor telling his mother that he was not going to live until the morning.

What do you do in that situation? It comes down to belief.

Erickson started putting every ounce of energy that he had to try to find if he could move any part of his body. He found he could blink his eyes a little bit. It took him another incredible amount of effort and time to get somebody's attention and get them to realize that it was a signal. And then it took him another intense amount of effort and time to set up a communication pattern. After many hours of intensive efforts he finally was able to get across the message that he wanted to get to his mother, which was to turn his bed towards the window so he could see the sun coming up the next morning.

I think that is part of what made Erickson who he was. Not the content of his life, but how he dealt with those challenges. And he kept that through all his life.

When I was down visiting him, he must have been about 75 or 76, and somebody asked him how long he expected to live. He answered, "Looking at it medically, I should make it until about 70."

That tells you something about his beliefs and attitudes.

I remember I was down there when I was about 20 years old. There was just me and another young man—his name was Jeffrey Zeig. At one point Erickson showed us this card that he had gotten from his daughter. On the front of the card there was this cartoon character who was standing on a tiny planet in the midst of the huge universe, and on the front of the card it said, "When you think of how huge and vast and complex the universe is, doesn't it make you feel kind of insignificant and small?"

When you opened up the card on the inside it said, "Me neither!"

This is the point about Erickson.

I don't think his power to heal came from his ability to give embedded commands or put people in hypnosis. In fact, my wife said of him when she visited him, "I read all the books on Erickson, did a bit of hanging around all the people who do Erickson's techniques. All these presuppositions in language patterns—I could hear all that stuff in what he was doing. In fact, I thought he was a lot more obvious about it than people like Richard Bandler or Steve Gilligan. But he had such rapport with you at such a deep level that I wouldn't have dreamt of not doing what he was asking, for fear that I might break that rapport."

That quality of rapport was Erickson's power.

If you get rapport with somebody on the level of identity you don't have to be indirect and sneaky. The power it creates when you believe in somebody else because you, like Erickson perhaps, have had your moments of truth and have reached inside to your identity and perhaps beyond, is enormous. It is what you believe about something that gives it its impact.

Perhaps you can take a moment and allow yourself to go back to your experiences in your life where you have been tested, where your beliefs have been tested, perhaps where your identity has been tested, or your survival, and where you have been able to reach deeply inside and find that belief that says, "Go for it!" As Jesus said, "He who has faith in a little has faith in a lot."

One of the nice things about N.L.P. is that you can get hold of something that maybe you only had for a brief glimmer in your life and you can make more of it. You can intensify it. You can

anchor it, even find the strategies behind it, and begin to take
these resources and those beliefs and that strength and that
identity and spread it to the parts of your life where you need it
the most like Linda did in the demonstration.

Continue going back to your history, to your experiences.
Perhaps you will find other resources as well; perhaps a special
friendship with a person that you least expected who
supported you at a time when you really needed it the most.
Find even the objects of your childhood that gave you pleasure
and were resources for you; perhaps a bicycle on which you
learned the resource of balance. Maybe you had some toy
musical instruments with which you learned the joy of making
noise and sound, perhaps a special doll.

Go back even further; maybe even back to when you first
learned to write the difference between big "A" and little "a",
"b", "c". Then learning that those letters went together to make
words and that the words were not a function of those letters,
but a function of the relationship between them. And those
words went together to make sentences, and the sentences
paragraphs. In the same way you learned to put together your
feelings. Those feelings were like letters and words. Perhaps
initially you were not sure what certain feelings meant, but you
learned how to give them a meaning. You learned how important it was to recognize pain as well as joy. And all those feelings fit together to make the sentences and the paragraphs that
made the story of your life.

Find the special feelings of your life, the ones that have been
the best guides; the ones that have guided you to your own
truth, to your own identity, and cherish those feelings. Whether
they feel good or bad, they have been your guides. Perhaps
they have changed, taking different meanings as you grew
older. Perhaps you left some feelings from your childhood
behind; feelings that you can take with you now only if it is

appropriate or ecological. Feelings that you can allow yourself to reexperience tomorrow or in the days to come.

I would like to make the transition to our next belief change process with a metaphor about a group of people who lived far away in space. These people are the opposite of us in how they live their lives. They watched us and decided we did it backwards; we're born, grow up, work hard all our lives, and die at the end.

So these people lived their lives in reverse order. They die first and get it over with. They spend the first few years of their lives in an old people's home, tired and weary of the world, seeming somehow distant from the people who are relatives or friends.

But as they grow older they actually grow younger. The more time they spend in the old people's home, the more connected they seem to become with their fellows; the more excited and the more recognition they have with their family.

Finally they get old enough to get out of the old people's home, and somebody gives them a gold watch and they go to work. At first in their work they feel they have done everything that they could. There are not really any new directions; they get weary and tired of their work. But the more time they spend in their work the younger they get; more creative ideas begin to come to them, the more interest they take, the more excited they get arriving at work every day.

Finally it seems like a wonderful adventure to go to work. When they reach that, they have to get out of work and go to college where they can spend time learning about themselves trying to find themselves.

In their world students sometimes protest for war, because they fight wars backwards from the way that we do it. They fly planes backwards over destroyed areas of land. As the plane flies over destroyed trees, homes, and people, it is almost as if it sends down a magical ray. And all that destruction becomes rolled up into a tiny ball, leaving behind it green trees and flowers and people and buildings. Then the plane sucks the little ball up into itself, and it flies over many areas rolling up the destruction to balls and pulling them inside itself.

Then the planes land backwards on an air strip. People come with little trucks and take the little balls of destruction to a factory. At the factory these balls are carefully disassembled and taken apart. People take all these parts in trucks and they bring them out to various places, where they put them back into the ground, where they can never hurt anybody again.

As these people continue to get younger, they go through a confusing time in their adolescence. They are not really sure of their identity. They have confusing experiences about who they are and their relationships to others. But since they have all their adult memories to remember forward to, they have resources that can help them through this time.

They can finally enter childhood, where each day their eyes open wider to the world around. Their sense of wonder and energy grows. Their beliefs seem to become broader, more open, more flexible each day. Then they spend the last nine months of their lives in a soft and warm environment where every need, every wish is taken care of for them. And they end it all up as the gleam in somebody's eye.

Sometimes I think it is useful to change the way we perceive our lives; to learn from dreams and in other ways. Perhaps tonight your own unconscious mind can surprise and delight you with some special gift, pleasant memory, or pleasant sensation. Maybe you can particularly enjoy somebody's company, or sharing a feeling or belief with somebody with the innocence of a child. And with that childish innocence, which is a very precious thing, perhaps you can find yourself coming back to this room, to this space with your eyes opening maybe a little wider, your senses a little more opened to the world, your energy a little bit higher for the things that are important for you.

CHAPTER III

BELIEF SYSTEMS AND CORE BELIEFS

Sometimes the limitation a person experiences comes from a belief system, not just a belief. In other words, you are not working with one belief; there are multiple beliefs feeding off each other.

In that case, you need to realize that you have to step back and look at the whole system of beliefs. The limitation may also come from a deeper, more core-level belief than a belief about capability. If a person starts with a belief that you are going to hurt him, and you sit there trying to separate out the parts of a synesthesia, this higher-level belief about your identity is going to have more effect than anything else you are doing. So you have to step back and ask, *"Where is the real limiting belief?"*

"Is it the one I am working on, or is it the one I keep bumping my head on every time I try to do something?

As Albert Einstein said, "Everything should be made as simple as possible but not simpler!"

In other words, if something takes precision and time, then that is what it takes. That is the commitment and investment that is appropriate to make. Trying to find a 'quick and dirty' way to change something that is a sophisticated and important issue is not necessarily the most appropriate strategy. Putting a band-aid on something that is infected is going to create more problems.

And that is what we are saying here. Use a band-aid if that is what it needs. But if there is an infection, then I need to treat the immune system.

This is important in N.L.P. I am not saying, "Everything should take a long time and be complicated," but *some things are worth spending time on, and worth doing fully with impeccability.*

So, *how do you detect a core belief? How do you know when you have a relevant belief? How do you find a belief to begin with?*

I can't always come up to someone and ask, "What is the core belief that is bothering you?"

How do we know that this belief is the core belief?

They say that changing beliefs is like the recipe for tiger stew. Step 1, you have to catch the tiger—that is the hard part! The rest is simple, like any other stew.

Perhaps the other issue to deal with at this point is:

How Are Beliefs Concealed?

The hardest part of trying to identify a belief is that the ones that affect you the most are typically the ones you are the least conscious of.

That is the first thing that you have to address when you are working with beliefs. There are four common problems in identifying beliefs. I will review them all, then we will go to some of the solutions.

1. The smoke screen

This is like what James Bond does when bad guys are approaching. You push the button and smoke comes out of the back of your car, allowing you to escape.

And very often, especially if the belief is associated with something very deep or painful, people are going to put up a smoke screen.

You are thinking that everything is going great. You are making all this progress; you are getting down to the core of the problem and all of a sudden the client goes blank or everything starts to get very vague and confusing.

You are getting right down close to their belief and that protective part of them pushes the button. And all of a sudden you find yourself lost and confused.

When you find this, you must realize this is not a bad thing. It only means that you are close. What I have people do very often *is to actually switch what they are doing and focus on the smoke—in whatever form it represents itself.*

- It could be just a feeling that comes up from nowhere like "I can't go any further." That could be a smoke screen.

- The smoke screen could be when all of a sudden somebody starts changing the subject and going irrelevant.

- In addition to just blanking out and becoming vague, sometimes everything shuts up inside the person. That could be a smoke screen. You have to realize that this is your doorway to the belief.

Ed Reese (another N.L.P. trainer) and I were working with a person who was trying to set some simple behavioral outcomes. Whenever we started trying to get a clear sensory-based statement of an outcome, however, he would get vague and fuzzy. It was almost like smoke. It would get hazy and he couldn't see anything. So we stopped going for the outcome and suggested, "Just watch that smoke for a moment, and focus on this smoke. And as you focus on that smoke, let it begin to clear and see what is really behind it."

All of a sudden he began almost convulsing and regressed into a very powerful state, a very powerful memory.

When he was nine years old he was playing baseball with some friends, and he was going to hit this ball as hard as he could. He was so concentrated on the ball and his goal that he didn't notice that the three-year-old brother of one of his friends was running behind him. He swung at the ball as hard as he could, gave it everything he had inside him, and missed it and hit this three-year-old boy in the head and killed him.

Now think of how that relates to his not being able to have an outcome: "When I set my goal and decide to really go for it I could miss and kill someone."

That was much more important than defining his goal. This experience had built a really limiting belief in this man at nine years old, when he didn't have the resources that he needed to fully make sense of it. And that wasn't necessarily the belief to build from what happened. That was a terrible thing that happened, but the belief doesn't have to be, "I should never try anything."

Looking beyond the smoke screen, you often find something that is much more important. We will come back in a moment to how to deal with this particular kind of situation. Let's go to the second issue in finding beliefs.

2. Red herring

A 'red herring' is a false clue.

In English murder mysteries, a red herring comes when the fugitive leaves a clue to purposefully lead the detective in a wrong direction.

Some therapists have the habit of inducing all their clients to tell about their mothers and their childhood, but that is not necessarily where the issue is. So the client learns to say, "He went that way!" when he's really going this way. It is like a smoke screen, because *it is protection of a part that doesn't want to be found out.*

When you think about it, a lot of people are trying to find the parts of themselves that they don't like so they can get rid of them. It is another way for a person to protect himself from pain by trying to hide out.

In business situations some people will have a "hidden agenda," as they call it, and they keep trying to hide this because they really have something else in mind. Maybe they are angry with you, but they are sitting there complimenting you, trying to get you to do something. It is important to recognize congruency in this case.

In all fairness, the person who is leaving the red herring is not necessarily lying. They might not even know it. It might be true that at one level they are satisfied, but at another level they are not. Or at one level this is the right clue, but at the other level it is not even close.

This red herring issue is one of the biggest problems in the coordination of the psychological and health professions these days. I remember recently reading two studies that came out the same month. One study claimed that they had proved conclusively that the attitude of patients affected their health. And the other study claimed that they proved conclusively that the attitude of their patients made no difference.

So I looked a little further into both of them. The one that proved that the attitude did affect health had judged the attitude of their patients based on participation in support groups and what kind of behavioral changes they made.

The other one based the identification of their patients' attitude judged by a pencil and paper self-evaluation.

Now, you realize that people who are seriously ill are probably the least able to evaluate their attitudes. It is like the persons who are the most drunk are the least able to evaluate their performances in driving. If you give them a self-evaluation test and ask, "How well can you drive?" they will say, "Perfectly." They will tell you that they never had better coordination in their lives.

The same thing happens with people who are seriously ill. If you ask them if they think they can get better, they will say, "Yes!" because they want to so much that they are not necessarily being honest with themselves.

The red herring often comes from incongruity.

The solution is to watch for all the cues, tone of voice, physiology, the minimal cues.

3. Fish in the dreams

This name comes from a radio comedy program where a comedian portrayed a psychoanalyst who had a theory that all people's problems could be traced to fish in their dreams. So when a client would come in he would ask, "Did you have any dreams last night?"

"Oh, I don't remember very well."

"Think about it. You must have had dreams."

Of course if he is a good patient he will find a way of going along with the doctor.

"If it will help me get well, then yes, I had a dream."

"Were there any fish in it?"

"No, I don't remember any fish. No, I don't think so."

"Well, what were you doing?"

"Walking down the sidewalk."

"Were there any puddles by the sidewalk?"

"I don't know."

"But there could have been?"

"Yes."

"Were there any fish in that puddle?"

"No, no."

"Were there any restaurants on this street?"

So the client finally admits there could have been a restaurant.

"Were they serving fish?"

"Yes, I guess they could have been serving fish."

"Good! That confirms my theory. I discovered it."

And you know, N.L.P. people could do the same thing. *Are you sure you are not making a picture at an unconscious level?*

People can draw all sorts of things out of their clients, especially when they are cooperative clients. They will confirm all theories.

I think that the resolution here is physiology again. You can't trust what people say, or what you think, so that really is when the *calibration of the minimal cues* comes in, setting up a behavioral demonstration, not talking about it, but running up right into the impasse, not being afraid of finding the impasse. The impasse is not failure, it is success.

4. Critical mass

The term critical mass comes from physics where, in order to create a chain reaction in electrons and atoms, you have to reach a certain threshold of energy. When you finally reach that level the chain reaction starts.

It is like the straw that breaks the camel's back. But sometimes, I see people grabbing this last straw and saying, "There must be something magic about this straw. I can prove it, it just broke my camel's back." Of course, if all the other straws hadn't been piled first, it wouldn't have made any difference.

Sometimes when I am working with somebody, I reframe several parts, change some fear with sub-modalities, confront a limiting belief, etc. Finally I anchor a resource and collapse the anchors. Then the person says, "Wow, now I feel wonderful!"

Then somebody in the audience raises his hand and asks why I didn't just do that resource anchor in the first place and skip the other stuff. It worked so well.

Of course, the reason it worked so dramatically is because all of the rest had built up to it.

The same will be true with belief. I need to find the beliefs and maybe work with more than one belief.

So realize that people don't necessarily get limited by a single belief. You are working with a system.

These are the issues that you want to keep in mind.

A belief is not "A" picture or "A" set of words or "A" feeling, but a relationship among all of them. And that is a different level of thinking.

The way in which we resolve a belief is not necessarily to try to get rid of the content, but to rearrange the relationships.

People can have the same experiences and respond very differently.

Core Beliefs

Work With Carla

Let's explore how to find a belief. The best way to do that is to have a demonstration. Let's take Carla.

Carla had stated there was something she was working on. This could make an interesting and instructive demonstration. First we have to keep in mind the four problems in finding beliefs: the Smoke Screen, the Red Herring or false clue, the Fish In Dreams, and finally the idea of Critical Mass or a group of beliefs all together in a system.

We want to find the impasse.

The Search For The Impasse

R.: Carla, we don't necessarily need to know the content, but I know there is this "thing" that keeps coming up and that you are imagining as a pain in your head. You tried to do things with it, but I think you said that even yesterday when you were thinking about doing the NLP exercises it would come up and stop you.

So what are the presenting problems or symptoms?

C.: *I have a pain in my head as if a revolver was shooting inside. It moves from here to there. I can't take it away.*

R.: Our first question is: Is this a function of belief? Or is this just a headache?

I assume that for you it represents something more than a regular headache. Has it been something that has been here for a long time? Or is it recent?

C.: *No, I already went through it before. It happens when "I HAVE TO."*

R.: When you have to do something?

C.: *Yes, but I like doing these things, but if I have to do them, I don't know how to go to them.*

R.: What you are saying is beginning to lead us to some fairly common issues. We have a sort of paradox; I want to do it, but I also have to do it somehow, and that is when this thing starts to come up.

By the way, I want to make a distinction in terms of elicitation. As we are working with any problem, we want to separate the symptoms from the cause.

The headache is the symptom.

The question is, *what is the cause of the headache?*

Many people have techniques to deal with symptoms but which fail to address the cause.

In other words, you can have pain control techniques or pain medicine, but if you don't treat the cause of the pain, then it will just come back.

When somebody wants to lose weight, the weight is only the symptom. It is not the cause.

The same thing is true in business. There are problems in business that are symptoms, and if you just patch up the symptom you haven't really made an overall change in the system in the way that you need to.

In our case, the symptom is a headache, and we want to find what causes it. Then we want to find out if it is a belief issue.

And if it is, what is the belief? Is it just one belief?

So we have this feeling as if somebody had a gun in her head.

Actually she said, "as if I had a gun in my head" and she made the gesture herself with her left hand.

(To Carla): What is this? Is there some part of you that is stopping you from going "ahead"?

C.: *No, I don't think so.*

R.: Where is this gun coming from?

C.: *If I don't aim at myself I aim at others.*

R.: That is an interesting statement. The interesting thing to me is that seems *an excessive sort of response to just feeling you have to do something.*

We find now a response that seems somewhat disproportionate to the issue that seems to be there. Let's move this way; this is something that has been there for a while; you had this at different times of your life.

We sort of have this interesting belief that *if I don't direct this pain or this gun at myself, I will direct it at somebody else.*

That certainly *qualifies as a belief.*

But we get the sense that it is not the whole belief.

There must be something else to this.

One of the things Freud said was that "belief repeats the history of its own origin." And I think one of the best strategies to use at this stage might be to search for the origin of this.

The question is, *how are we going to find the origin of it?*

As I said, the first thing that we want to get to is the impasse. So what I want to do is trace this *thing* back, but I have to find what I want to *trace* first.

Do I want to trace *the pain* back, the *have to* back, or *the belief* that if I don't inflict this on myself I will inflict it on others?

What I want to do even before getting to that stage is to take a moment and search for the impasse.

(To Carla): When you have this feeling or pain you probably have a lot of resources. You know that you don't have to do things that you don't want to do. Logically, you know that you don't have to.

C.: *It is not logical. If I could get it with logic, then I would because I really enjoy what I do.*

R.: Why don't you just drop the headache and 'gun' then?

C.: *It is as if I had a hook put in my head and as if somebody wanted to pull on it every time I want to do what I like. It is as if I were pulled back.*

R.: Listen to this: "Every time I want to do something that I like then I am pulled back." This is not an uncommon problem for lots of people. The fact that I want to do it is what triggers me holding me back.

Have you tried letting it go? What did you try to do about it?

C.: *When I want to have access to what I like doing, I close my eyes and make myself as tiny as possible so I won't be seen leaving. But this thing is so smart that it always catches me back.*

R.: You noticed that she is talking about "this thing." When we think about identity what she is saying is that there is that other identity in me. It is an "it."

C.: *Or I have to stay very still, so I can pretend that I am not doing that thing I enjoy doing. It especially occurs because of the fact that I am in theater and I create plays for children. I can only go and listen to my intuition and just do it. But I can't decide or think about doing it. I can't have access to it, I can only undergo. I can't stand back in order to think about it and put things together.*

R.: Let's get a behavioral example. Something that you would like to do.

C.: *Singing.*

R.: What would you like to sing?

C.: *It is not singing a song, it is just sounds.*

R.: Can you do that right now?

C.: *I can do that. But I can't go any further.*

I can do all these things. I know that I am meant for that, but I can't realize it.

R.: What happens if I ask you to go ahead and do it, right now?

C.: *I could do it but I would be afraid.*

R.: (To group): What I want is to go further and further in creating that impasse.

(To Carla): Well, take that next step!

You say that when you want to do something that you like, you can't because you have this hook. Well, I want to see this hook. *I don't want to follow a red herring.*

So let's identify something that would be really nice for you to do, that you really want to do, and we will just start going for it.

C.: *I am able to do things by impulse, but thinking things over and doing them quietly, that I am totally unable to do.*

R.: So let us think about this. It is an interesting kind of paradox because it is thinking about it, not doing it.

And that will sometimes fool people.

The problem is not in the behavior.

If you try to find any particular behavior, she will say, "It is not the problem, I can do that." What you are beginning to hear is that at an outcome level, she can probably get any particular outcome. She says, "When I do it *for me* this is when the problem comes in."

That means to me that this is more at the level of identity.

This is thinking about "what I want to do and what I would like."

And that is something that I would like you to do right now—think about some things you would like for yourself.

C.: *Doing or being?*

R.: Being.

C.: *What I would like to be? To be a good transition inside, to hear rhythms and sounds. Let them come in from outside, play with them inside, and return them to the outside differently, share them with the others, and teach them to others.*

R.: I see that *you can think about this and it doesn't seem to bother you.*

C.: *No, it always fills me with joy.*

R.: Again, where is the problem?

C.: *I can't! I don't know. I don't know what!*

R.: Is it happening right now?

C.: *Is what?*

R.: This problem!

C.: *There is something missing. Maybe I don't take the responsibility for what I would like to be.*

R.: Again, just to review where we are; *we are trying to find out where the symptom occurs, and how it becomes an impasse.* What you first find is that it is a little slippery because it is not just at the level of the behavior. It is not, "I want to have this behavior and I can't get there."

It is sort of, "If I want to get ready to do it, I can't." I find a lot of people who have great behavioral competence. They do all kinds of things quite well actually, and yet their beliefs are that they are not doing them well. Of course, nobody takes them seriously because they wonder, what real problem does this person have?

They can do everything. They are competent, but that is not the issue. The issue is, what is it like on the inside for the person? What I hear Carla saying is "I can do it if I don't take responsibility for it, but if I take responsibility for it I can't do it."

(To Carla): Can you take responsibility?

C.: *When I have to take the responsibility, I can't take it. I don't know how to and I can't get rid of "I have to." I can't turn it to my benefit because it is taken away from me after, during and before it. I feel that sucking out, but only on this side.*

R.: I think we are getting close to the impasse. She is using some of the same gestures and voice tones she's used earlier. It seems like we have discovered a pattern. This is what I'd like to do next.

The Time Line: Associated With Time

(Robert will use two types of voice, his normal voice to talk to the audience and a soft, very slow, hypnotic voice to talk to Carla.)

R.: Carla, I would like you to imagine that in front of you, here on the floor, there is a line. This line is your line of

PAST   PRESENT   FUTURE

Figure 13. Time Line

time. To the left is the past, to the right is the future, that is, where you would like to be able to go, and to the left is what has happened. Here you are in the present and you have this thing, something that is sucking part of your identity out.

I am going to ask you in a moment to step on this imaginary line, facing your future, and I would like you to *put your awareness on this sucking you out, on this 'gun.'* Then I want you to start walking backwards along this line, back in time.

And whether it is conscious or not, notice which events of your life are associated with this feeling.

I would like you to go back through your life until you find an event, or a set of events, when this 'sucking out' started.

And when you step on that line, I want you to be fully inside your life experiences.

(To audience): In other words, there are two basic kinds of time perception, *through time* and *in time. Through time* is when you look at your life disassociated. *I can be outside looking at the events of the past, looking at the future*, or *I can step* into time *and* relive it, relive a particular experience.

(To Carla): I am going to ask you to step on this line and, as you go back, to be reliving the events of your life as you go, until you find the earliest experience associated with that sucking out of who you are.

(Carla steps on the time line and starts to walk backward.)

R.: You can close your eyes. This is the present, right now. As you stand here, the future is in front of you, and your past is behind you. Then you are going to slowly start walking to your past. Each step back is going to take you through events of your life bound together by this thread, by this gun, by this sucking. As you find any event that is important with respect to that, you can stop and notice it...and be in it.

(To the audience): Now, I ask you all out there to *watch for physiology changes*.

(To Carla): Keep allowing yourself to move backwards in time; each step closer, closer to that incident at that time.

C.: *I can't know. I have no right to know.*

R.: (To the audience): That is one belief right there. "I have no right to know."

C.: *I have no right to say that I know.*

R.: Notice this is even different. By the way, if you have noticed where her accessing cues have been, whenever she thinks about the problem state, her eyes have been down on the left (internal dialog).

C.: *In any case I will never be able to know, because I am not allowed to. If I know, I am betraying and I don't know what I am doing wrong. I pretend that I know nothing.*

R.: I am going to ask you to keep going back, *but without having to know*, you are going to go back to it.

C.: *I have nothing to do?* (visibly shaking) *I am scared.*

R.: I want you to notice that feeling and know that feeling is alright, and notice what else is happening. Then I want you to take a step back before that ever happened.

C.: *I have to jump over something.*

R.: That is alright. So jump.

(Carla jumps over an imaginary obstacle.)

R.: Now you are back before that ever happened.

C.: *I can still see it coming.*

R.: Alright, then take a step before that can ever reach you, or rather see it going in the future that way, so it goes in front of you into the future. You are standing before that event happened, looking at it, and it is going off in the future.

C.: *It is as if I had to come before my birth, as if I was born to undergo this.*

R.: So let us take a step back to before your birth.

C.: *Then I would be free.*

(Relieved laughter in the audience)

(Carla laughs.) I must go out of my mother.

R.: Now from there, you can look at this event that will happen, but you are outside of it. You are at a place before that ever happened.

C.: *When I did step out my headache went away and now that I have to see it far ahead of me, as to get rid of it, it goes, "no, no." It goes away and I feel free. But now that I have to face it again, it comes back straight away.*

R.: OK. First stop for the moment and stay free of "it"; step back and don't look at the event.

C.: *But it is coming back. I don't know how to stay away. It is the same thing when I want to sneak out to create without anybody knowing it. If I become aware of it, it comes.*

R.: First, I just want you to get to a place where you are free of it for a moment; maybe if you step back further.

C.: *Because you said it, everybody knows it. So it comes back to get me. It even gets me in the dark.*

R.: I want you to step to a place where it can't catch you, it can't come. Think about it this way, from where you are, looking at this future place on your time line: that event hasn't happened yet. It doesn't even have to happen.

C.: *I can't do that because it is drawing me there. I am willing to do it, but I don't know how.*

R.: What belief would you need in order to be able to do it? What is the belief that you would need to free you?

C.: *I would have the right to be what I am, and it would be alright.*

R.: (To the audience): This certainly is a belief about identity, about worthwhileness. (One of the three types of problems about beliefs is precisely the fact that you believe you are not worth it, that you don't deserve it.)

C.: *That I don't have to pay for someone, or for people.*

R.: "I have the right to be what I am." I want to find out if here, before that happened, you had the right to be who you are.

C.: *I did, but I have the feeling that this thing is always so much more clever that it will always get behind me. Or I have to run ahead faster and faster endlessly, and it always gets behind me.*

R.: What would happen if you had the right to be who you are?

C.: *I would turn back and get rid of this thing.*

R.: Can you literally 'turn back' on your time line and get rid of that thing behind you?

(Turns Carla to face prebirth experience on time line.)

C.: *It is calming down inside. It still hurts but I can cope with it.*

R.: What you are facing now is way before your life; this *thing* is behind you. As you look back this way at the event can you see, *"Yes, I have the right to be what I am"*?

C.: *As soon as there is light I am caught like in a sandwich, and as soon as I have access to anything, it kills it. I have the feeling that I am willing to do what you are asking me to do; I want to get out of this, but I am trapped from everywhere. This thing is a lot smarter than you!*

(Laughter in the audience)

R.: We shall see! I like the challenge. I think we have finally found the impasse! First, please come out of this line now for a moment. This thing doesn't know what I can do yet! I haven't even started to do anything with it.

We have been finding the impasse here.

This is a classic example of belief, and you can see how it works.

I wanted you to get to the impasse. What you have been experiencing and describing is an impasse.

C.: *It is coming at me from all directions.*

R.: It has nothing to do with behavior. I mean, all these feelings and thoughts have nothing to do with reality as we know it.

C.: *Being trapped wherever I am in time. It follows me anywhere.*

R.: But what is it?

For me, what is happening here is a good example of an identity-related belief. *It doesn't necessarily have to do with the concrete world of external reality, it has to do with the internal world of your own identity.*

Through Time

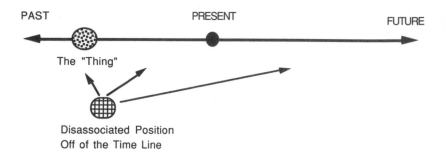

Figure 14. Viewing the Negative Event 'Through Time'

R.: Now from out here, *off* this line, I want you to see all the things we did. There was this fear. There was this *thing* you had to jump over, and you got back to here. For a moment you took a step before that and you were free.

Then you thought about it and it came. You turned this way towards a more distant past and it got better, but then it sandwiched you again. I want you to see it all from outside. OK?

Where does this *thing* come from? Does it come from back there or does it come from somewhere here, and is it just able to go all around?

(Robert points at some places on the time line.)

C.: *I think it is coming from somewhere here (the negative experience), and then it sticks behind me. But it hides and as it sticks to me wherever I go, with my mind or body, it follows me. I have the feeling that it is like a leech. If I take it off, either it comes twice as hard and I will be covered until I am completely exhausted, or I take it off, crush it, kill it. I run away very quickly, and when I get where I want to go, I find it there waiting for me.*

R.: Now you begin to hear the kinds of things that will happen with the belief, the ways it is operating for her, the impasse.

Before I proceed, notice now that *we are getting a dissociated representation* of it.

When she was on the line, she was more caught inside of it. Now coming outside of all this, she is in a different relationship to it.

In here, I wanted her to be associated inside of it. Out here we are dissociated from it, looking at it.

That gives us two perspectives, two positions.

She said something else very important when she was in here associated on her time line: *It is more clever than you.*

This has a really important significance in two ways.

1) It is a statement about her relationship to me.

She is saying that there has to be trust in the relationship here with me in order to do anything there with that negative event.

In other words, she has got a problem that has been bothering her for a lifetime. I'm supposed to help her.

Very often people in such a situation will appropriately say, "You think you can help me with this? I am going to put YOU inside of it. I am going to put this belief on you and see how you handle it. You think you can do better than me? Here, I will do it to you."

That is a legitimate thing. And I meant it when I said we hadn't even started with it yet!

2) This *"thing"* is something that is a belief on a particular level.

You have to be clever on that level. It is not a level of logic; it is a level of belief.

The Meeting Of The Two Parts

In other words, Carla's statement is telling us two things. It is a statement about what type of resources we will need in order to resolve the problem, and it is also a statement about the relationship that I have with my subject, and that relationship is important.

Either one of these could deepen the impasse. She said, "I wish I could do what you say," and yet the other part of her is in here saying, "Oh yeah?" *I need to have a relationship with both.*

Obviously the missing "thing" here, the "it," is the other part of her. It's what, all her life, she has tried to pull off, squash, get rid of. And it is not going anywhere; it is a part of her identity.

(To Carla): It is not a non-part of you, it is a part of you.

That is why you are never going to get away from it; that is what it is telling you.

The question is, what are you going to do about it?

C.: *With who? What?*

R.: With this part of you that nags you.

C.:　*It's me?*

R.:　I don't know if you have ever considered that before.

C.:　*What? I don't understand a thing here.*

R.:　Yes, I believe you! Do you hear what she is saying? She doesn't understand now. This has always been the other, not her.

I think this is part of you.

And the question is not how to get rid of it, but what part it plays in your life. We can tell that there was something that happened back here that was very frightening in a lot of ways.

At this time something happened in which this part either developed, or maybe was split out.

We want to find out how to fit this back together into a new relationship that is going to be useful and strong, rather than something that is going to keep you in a double bind.

(To audience): She will always feel something is missing.

If I try to leave that other part of me behind, it is missing. It is a whole part of me and my life that I am ignoring.

Here is where we get to *the system of beliefs*.

From there in the present, it's, "I can't know, I can't talk about it."

Here in the past, it's, "I can't get rid of it."

That is a hell of a set of beliefs: *I can't get rid of it, I can't know it, and I can't talk about it.* These are the beliefs we need to be working with.

I think that by the time we get done, you will see that this is a classic example of beliefs of this kind. It will illustrate some very important points about beliefs.

By the way, we have already started to make some interventions. I actually began to establish a different belief already, didn't I?

From out here, I said that the problem is that it is a part of her; something that she never really considered before. Notice: that is a belief that is at a different level from her other beliefs. It is not, "I can't get rid of it, I can't talk about it." Rather, I am asking her to believe, "It is ME, my identity."

C.: *If I hear a happy thing in there, and if it is mine I will take it!*

R.: Notice that when she was talking about not being able to get rid of "all this", she was using her left hand. Now she is using her right hand.

I think you can begin to see the asymmetry.

How The System Works

(Carla is still off of her time line.)

R.: Let's take a moment to explore; I would like you to do it from out here. What happened in here in this place on your time line where "it" came from?

I think you could see that when she approached that place she was shivering, and I don't think she was pretending.

Can you see a dissociated image of what happened in there?

C.: *No, because I went through with closed eyes and I can't*
     see and I don't want to see. But I would like to see now.

R.: (To audience): I think you are getting my point about the
     two parts of her identity. Do you hear a little conflict in
     that statement?

     (To Carla): I think there is a part of you that sees and a
     part that doesn't see.

     What resource would you need to be able to see that event
     from out here?

C.: *I would need to see from a distance, and I wish it were*
     not me who sees it. I would need to be able to act as if it
     was not me who was seeing me.

R.: Do you hear this? This is probably exactly what she does
     believe in order to exist without knowing what happened.

     How old were you then?

C.: *Between four and seven.*

     (To the audience): Obviously, something traumatic hap-
     pened to this child between four and seven. When you are
     between four and seven you have a lot more flexibility in
     your identity.

     How does a child go about dealing with a traumatic
     event?

Two very common strategies are:

1. I will make it so it didn't happen to me, it happened to
   somebody else.

2. I will make it so that it is not me who is remembering it or
   seeing it happen.

Either one creates an interesting issue.

"I can't ever resolve it, because I am not really seeing it. That is not me who is really seeing it. Or if I see it, that is not really happening to me."

I think you begin to hear how identity issues can influence you.

(From here, Robert will emphasize the dissociation and work with sub-modalities, as you would do with a phobia in order to get closer to the incident).

> (To Carla): But what if we had another choice from out here, if we put some kind of a screen here so that what you are watching was more like a movie. Maybe you can even make it fuzzy enough so you don't see exactly who is who in it. Maybe it is even like a black and white silent movie, and you can run it very quickly.
>
> All I am concerned about here is who **is involved in that movie. I don't even care what happened.**

C.: *I have the feeling I am making up the pictures.*

R.: That is alright.

C.: *Maybe I am making it all up.*

R.: That is a really powerful statement. *I feel that maybe I just made it all up.*

> Of course, that is another protection strategy: "Either it didn't happen to me, or I just made it up." Is it a "red herring" or not?
>
> What do you see?

C.: *It's me.*

R.: Who else?

C.: *A man.*

R.: Anybody else? Your mother? Parents? Just you and this person?

C.: *There is me and that person with other people around in the house, always behind doors and walls.*

R.: They are there, but do they know what is going on, or don't they know?

C.: *They don't know; then they know so they try to find out.*

R.: **When does it end?** I want you to run it through to when it is over.

C.: *Because I have power at one point, it lasts for several years.*

R.: The other people who are in the house, who try to find out: When do they try to find out? Only at the end of all those years, or at each time?

C.: *Towards the end; there are other children, too, and they know earlier.*

R.: But they can't do anything?

C.: *They think it is fun, and I do too.*

R.: This is interesting. Is that the only belief that you have about it?

C.: *About what?*

R.: About this event, about what is happening there.

C.: *I am lying.*

R.: To whom?

C.: *To myself.*

R.: What about?

C.: *I pretend that I know nothing.*

R.: You don't know what?

C.: *That I love or like it.*

R.: So you have found there is a part of you that likes it, and a part of you that thinks it is not right?

C.: *I didn't say it wasn't right. It is the gaze of others, of adults, that say it.*

R.: It is the gaze of the grown-ups?

C.: *It is their gaze, not their words.*

R.: (To the audience): Did you hear what she said? It is in their gaze, not in their words.

C.: *Because they know, but they can't believe it, and they don't dare speak about it. I feel abandoned because of that.*

R.: We are starting to begin to unravel this, and what we want to do is to put in some resources now.

Here we have a situation where there is not just one belief, not one thing going on, but maybe more like three or four. "With the other children it is fun. I am lying to myself, not admitting that I like it."

What am I saying on the other side? Am I saying that I don't like it? Is that the lie?

C.: *I don't say anything.*

R.: So by not saying anything I am lying? By not saying anything I am engaging in lying?

C.: *Yes.*

R.:   (To the audience): Notice that auditory accessing here. The verbal elements seem to be associated with herself or the other children. The adults come in as the gaze. But they don't speak and that makes her feel abandoned by them.

The adults know but they can't believe it. Of course, there is one other person, there is the man who is involved, what about this person?

C.:   *He is... an adult I like very much.*

R.:   So this is somebody that you like. What is his belief? Does he gaze like the others? Does he lie to himself like you lie to yourself? Does he think it is fun like the other children?

C.:   *He acts as if he was playing.*

R.:   He acts as if he was playing, but he doesn't say anything to the other adults either?

C.:   *No, he is playing.*

R.:   (To the audience): So let's review what we have now.

Earlier we took a molecule of sensory representations and broke it apart into the different senses that were interacting. Here we have another molecule, but this molecule is not the same size or type as the earlier ones we were working with.

This is a molecule of identities and of beliefs in a relationship.

There was a relationship of all kinds of people back here. It is like a molecule of identities.

I think that in some way or another, Carla identified with each part of the system:

A part of her is **the gaze of the adults who abandoned her.**

A part of her is **the child who is lying to herself.**

A part of her is maybe **the man who is 'just playing.'**

A part of her is **the other children having fun and secrets.**

I think that the reason it follows her everywhere is because the answer is not about *doing* anything in particular here. The answer is not one single thing that we can bring to one single person here.

What makes it so compelling is that the system feeds on itself; everybody's behavior is supporting each other to maintain a dysfunctional system.

It is a lie upon a lie upon a lie upon a lie. Everybody is lying to themselves. The man is lying, the little girl is lying, the adults are lying; not because they are doing it on purpose, but because they can't help themselves.

My question is, **What are the resources needed to change that system?**

What are the resources needed by a four- to seven-year-old who came upon a situation that requires a great wisdom to understand what it means about her?

(To Carla): I think that perhaps now you might have the wisdom that allows you to solve it. Maybe not just the wisdom, but the courage and maybe some other resources.

C.: *I think I can do that.*

R.: (To the audience): **From out here, Carla has a different belief now.**

"From out here" doesn't mean that if we get back on that line she is going to maintain this same new attitude and that is what we have to integrate: the associated and dissociated identities.

C.: *What I use to work with children is the joy and pleasure of that little girl, but not the one in that situation. No, the other one. So I keep trying to avoid it. She is not free.*

R.: Because it has been a part of you that we really need to acknowledge just now. It has been a part of you that has never given up. A part of you that follows you everywhere. It says, "I am not going to let you forget, you can't forget. This is something important in life."

This was real. I don't even care about whether the content was true or not. **What is real are the relationships and the lying between the people.** What is real is what it can do to somebody. There is that part of you that knows that.

Imprint Theory

There is a standard N.L.P. technique, called **changing personal history,** in which you take a resource back into a person's past. Usually you take a capability that the person did not have as a child but has developed as an adult.

However, we have a situation here that is different from what would be solved by changing your own capabilities, because **the issue is not so much what resource you individually needed as much as it is the resource that the system needed.** We need to heal the relationship, not just the individuals.

A number of years ago I was doing some seminars with Timothy Leary (it had nothing to do with drugs). Leary got interested in N.L.P. because he thought it had more potential than

LSD to make certain changes. Maybe he was right! Part of the reason he had been interested in LSD to begin with was because he felt that it could put the brain into a state that could be reprogrammed and could help reprogram what he called **imprints.**

An imprint is not just some traumatic event from your personal history. An imprint is **a belief** or an **identity-forming experience**. It doesn't have to be traumatic. It is a reflection on your identity. The process of *reimprinting* derives from this work with Leary.

The word "imprint" comes from the late **Konrad Lorenz,** who studied ducklings from the time they hatched. He found out that when ducklings first hatched, for about a day or so, they would look for a 'mother-figure.' The ducklings searched for only one particular sub-modality to define their mother. All the mother had to do was to move. If something moved the ducklings would follow it.

They would follow Lorenz around while he was walking, for instance. After a day or so the duckling would have completed this imprint of the mother. After the imprint period was up, if you brought back the real mother they would ignore her and, for example, end up following around this old Austrian gentleman. So he walked around with little ducklings following him. When he got up in the morning, instead of being out in their nest, they would be all curled up on the porch around his wading boots.

They even imprinted one of these ducklings to a balloon. They pulled it around and the duckling followed it.

When this duckling that was imprinted to a balloon became an adult, it wouldn't court or mate with members of its own species. Instead it would go through all this courting behavior and try to mate with anything round.

This shows that when the duckling grew up the imprint of the mother also transferred into the imprint for a mate.

I think, as Leary did, that this happens to a certain degree in human beings.

If a female child has been physically abused by her father, the imprint, when she grows up, will create an interesting pattern. In spite of what she wants to do, or what she knows logically, she will often get herself into abusive relationships, because that imprint is like an archetype for how the relationship with a man should be.

If a female child has been abused by her mother, when she grows up she might somehow wind up abusing her own children and hate herself for it, but she won't know why. This means that your early experiences don't only affect your feelings, they create very deep role models for relationships.

There are certain transitions in life when you are compelled to take on that role. Whether you like the role or not, it may be the only role that you have. You go to *second position* with the role model. You step into their shoes in a way.

The power of this deep role modeling process first really struck me when I was working with a woman who had cancer of the throat. She was at a very powerful impasse in her recovery process, and finally blurted out, "I feel like my throat has been taken away from me. My body isn't mine."

So I had her put her attention on that feeling and go back into her history. She suddenly regressed into a very early memory. This is the way she described it: "I am a little girl; and my mother is holding me and she is shaking me." But all of her physiology as she said this was of the aggressive mother, not the helpless child. Her voice was full of anger and violence. I thought, "She's not regressing into a little girl." With that behavior she was regressing into the mother who is shaking the little girl.

You are not going to resolve this experience by bringing a resource only to the little girl. All her neurology is organized around the mother; she is being the mother. A typical change history wouldn't deal with that. **She incorporated the role of the mother into herself.** Whether it is something you like or dislike, you will incorporate roles learned from significant others.

Psychoanalysts talk about this as **identification with the aggressor.**

In order to build a model of the world, you also build models of significant other people. When you build a role model it is possible to *associate into* it. Especially if they had an influence on your identity.

Then that can become a very powerful organization in your own life. You see, when you are a child, you identify yourself with one role in a family system. What happens when you become the adult?

Who are you?

As one woman, who had been physically abused by her mother, put it to me, "When I was little and remembered these events, I always identified with the child; I was afraid. Now, because I am an adult, when I remember it, physically it is easier to identify as a mother. I can't be the child anymore. So I experience the rage and anger as well as the fear. I am an adult now, and I am the mother and I am the child."

> (To Carla): What I say is that the enemy is not the people who are stuck in a dysfunctional system. **You are not going to solve abuse by abusing the abusers.** You are just going to take on what they did. The 'enemy' is the system,

it is the relationship. **And you can't kill or shoot a relationship with a gun.**

That is not how to solve it. It is not necessary to believe, "I have to shoot myself or somebody else."

The question is not to use "reblaming" to keep putting the blame somewhere else. It is, "What is really going to solve the dysfunctional relationship?"

This has fear, this has rage, this has liking, fun and secrets. It has disbelief and denial. There is a whole system of things here, and our point to Carla is that this imprint is not going to go away, it is a part of you. And right now this imprint is not a conscious part of your mission. This part of you is not going to let you go forward into life and ignore or repress that time in your life that taught you so much about human beings and yourself.

C.: *I thought about this. I try to do exercises to get rid of it. Then there is another part of me that says that I am not honest, because I have the feeling that I don't want to get rid of it.*

R.: What she is saying is that a part of her wants to go on and wants to get rid of it. And Carla, I say thank God there is a part of you that doesn't want to be dishonest. And that part of you is important.

The next question is, if we are not going to solve this by killing people or putting them in prison or whatever, **what do you do with somebody like this man?**

This, I think, is *what the message and belief of N.L.P. are all about.*

I really have no right to tell Carla that she *should* have a resource available that will resolve this situation. If I would provide a resource, it must be at least as powerful and compelling as what is going on in that system. People worry about N.L.P. as being manipulative. But **if you don't have something that is at least as powerful as shooting a gun, then you have no right to propose an alternative.**

We have to have the tools, the techniques, the beliefs that can blow the dysfunctional system away. I don't necessarily mean to get rid of it, but **find a solution that makes it healthy.**

(To Carla): You have known for a long time that this is not healthy, and your own brain won't let you try to continue in an unhealthy way. It won't let you keep making more and more of the hiding and the deceit that happened here.

C.: *Things get mixed up here, because the pleasure I had in that situation is the same as the one I have in creating shows. So I can't have that pleasure and the creative pleasure.*

R.: Again you see the double bind. Here **is the imprint for the criterion of "pleasure."**

If I have pleasure, then I am recreating this negative relationship somehow. I don't want it to be unhealthy to experience pleasure in creating.

Is it the pleasure that made it unhealthy?

To me that is not what makes this system unhealthy. This is not the belief that I have about it. What I am saying is that **the enemy isn't in pleasure, the enemy isn't you.**

What is it then? There are a number of people in this system, any one of whom I think that Carla can identify with. As long as she is going to identify with them, let's go ahead and use it.

Part of what I was saying was that people identify with their parents. I know that when people have problems with their parents, it often only intensifies after their parents die. It obviously has nothing to do with the real parents. In fact, the reason it becomes more intense after the parents die is because you have to completely internalize that part of the system.

Therefore we need to solve Carla's problem from all parts of the system she has internalized. To me it is not any one of those that caused the problem; it is that something was missing from the system—from the relationship.

Something was missing in that man. Something was missing in that little girl. She did the best she could based on what she had. Something was missing in the children and friends. That little girl was abandoned.

C.: *It is just coming to me now that when you say that something is missing in the little girl and other children:* **I want to protect them; I say that is not true and...**

R.: Before we go any further, if you say "that is not true," *does that protect them? Are you protecting them?* Or are you going to be like those adults who are keeping that happening?

So how are you going to really protect her?

C.: *As what? As an adult?*

R.: Let's define that right now. She says, "I want to protect the little girl," but by doing what? By promoting the lie, by saying, "That isn't true?" Is that going to protect her?

C.: *No. It is the parents who must protect her.*

R.: So. Now we get to the parents.

What do those parents need in order to be really able to protect the little girl?

You see, she sort of repeats what the parents did: disbelief. "It isn't true." That is just going to keep the scar there.

What did the parents need that they didn't have?

(To Carla): Is that the way you think parents should act? Is that what *you* would do to another child who had that problem? What would you do? What resource would you have?

C.:   *First, I would* **be careful.** *My mother knew this. My mother knew that this man was like this. But she didn't watch this man and she didn't keep me away or warn me. She only hoped that it wouldn't happen, then was ashamed that it could happen.*

R.:   What resource would we need to bring to your mother, that she didn't have, so that she would have done something much, *much earlier* in that particular situation?

You said that what you would have done is to be attentive.

Notice that *that is the description of a result of a capability.* I am going to climb all those levels, because I think you need them all.

In order to be attentive, *what do you need* **to be capable of?** What do you know that your mother didn't know, so you wouldn't act the way she did towards a child?

C.:   *I am not afraid of this reality facing me and inside me.*

R.:   She actually *jumped up a level* (i.e., above capability level) *to a belief: "I am not scared to admit this,"* but I think that this solution also requires something on the identity level. What would your mother have needed inside to be able to say that?

C.: *Facing reality.*

R.: *What resource would she need to face it, what would she need inside?* Have there been times, even if it is not this, when you faced the reality of a situation?

C.: *Yes.*

R.: I want you to think of what was inside you that allowed you to do that. I want you to experience that.

C.: *I trusted my strength.*

R.: What I want you to do is, from out here, find that event on your time line where you really trusted your strength. Then step into that event and *really access that strength inside of you.* (Carla steps onto her time line). I want you to be really in touch with that trust in your strength.

And I would like to have you do this from here; *make an energy, or a color,* out of that feeling, that trust, that strength, where it comes from inside you.

Then I want you to shine it onto your mother in that memory. So from here you are giving her that light, that force, that trust.

And I want you to watch what she would do in that situation, if she had this resource that you have.

C.: *First she is all of a sudden very angry because she is found out. I can't do that. My legs are weak.*

R.: I want you to see what she does. Just watch. Let her do it for the moment. What does she do?

C.: *She looks at me wondering where I get that strength from.*

R.: She is looking at you here?

I first want you to use your strength before she knows where you get it from; instead of looking at you, have her *look at that system and do what she needs to do there.*

What is she going to do now that she has this strength and trust?

C.: *She is quietly going to talk to that man and tell him that she knows what he is up to.*

R.: What will happen?

C.: *She loves this man, but she says that she will do anything in her power, and she knows that she can...*

R.: Go on. Take your time.

(long silence)

C.: *... to protect her daughter and that he ought to know.* (Carla weeps softly.)

R.: What does he do when she says that?

C.: *He is in peace, because he is very young himself too, and there is nobody to acknowledge this for him, because such things don't exist in that family, because he is that himself. He only understands that he is wrong. He doesn't think of my mother as a threat. It is something that brings peace to him, that leads him to find his way.*

R.: Do you see how much more powerful that is than any gun you are going to find?

C.: *Yes.*

R.: What does the little girl learn when the mother does that?

C.: *If it happens at the very beginning, she plays with her cousins who are around, but in fact she wanted to experiment with that and... I don't know anymore.*

R.: Alright, she wants to experiment?

C.: *Not too much.*

R.: Before we go to the little girl, I want to find out if her mother had this strength. How did she react and interrelate with the little girl who wants to experiment?

C.: *She explains to her that there are lots of pleasures in life, that there are pleasures for little ones and pleasures for grown-ups. I am not sure that the little girl could have understood, but the mother would have made her understand it; that the little girl is a woman.*

R.: I want you to look at the little girl looking at her mother and listening to the strength in the voice of her mother. *How does she respond? Does she understand?*

C.: *She first is ashamed, but her mother smiles, takes the little girl in her arms...*

R.: What happens?

C.: *It is warm... it is soft... it is clear, lots of laughter, but gentle laughter. First, lots of peace and the little girl goes on playing. She is still sometimes afraid of that man because she still wants it.*

R.: But since the mother has the strength and talked to the man?

C.: *I have already forgotten that. The man has changed. I am not quite convinced that he has changed when I look around.*

Re-Association To The Time line

R.: First of all, we have that man here and she says, "I am not sure that I am convinced."

I want to take what we have just done one more step. Part of the reason why she might not be convinced is *because we have done all this from the event outside so far.*

In order to finish this part we are going to take this trust and strength, and *I am going to have you step onto the line into your mother.* You are going to step into her role, and see the little girl and see that man.

And I want you to go through associated. You can do it on the inside, you don't necessarily have to do it aloud.

But I want you to go through what you saw her doing, as if you were her doing that with the child, and with the man.

I want you to first take this resource, this strength. *Once again access that strength in yourself.*

(Robert anchors.)

C.: *I am scared again.*

(Robert anchors again. His voice has changed. He is speaking to the mother now.)

R.: That's alright. Take that feeling and that light and that voice and then step into it. Drop your mask and you can talk to that man that you love. You can let him know that you are going to do everything in your power to protect your daughter and he ought to know that, even though you have acknowledged your feelings for him.

You can do that in a way that gives him peace, because he can admire your strength and learn from you. And you can feel your strength, and it grows when you talk to him because you can see that he likes it. He needs to feel that strength too.

Then you can turn to your daughter and you can talk to her.

And she can find peace in your strength. Then go up this line to the present, because that little girl needed to know that you, the mother, wouldn't only do it that one time. The man may need more of that kind of talking in order to really change him. And your daughter needs more of that kind of talking to know she has not been abandoned. It has been said that communication is short term learning and that learning is long term communication. I think there is a lot of truth to that.

I would like you to *walk through time as the mother with that strength all the way to the present.*

Take your time. Be there next to that daughter as she grows up, sharing and communicating that strength. Just take your time to walk up to the present.

C.: *Lots of memories are coming back to me. This little girl, while she was growing up, did as many stupid things as she could and as hard as she could.*

R.: But if the mother had been there with her trust and strength and the ability to communicate, those might have developed very differently. That is what you can do now.

(Carla laughs. Her face is beaming. She walks with confidence now.)

You don't have to do it either quickly or slowly. Go at whatever rate or speed is appropriate as you walk up to the present through those memories, as you put them in order.

(Carla walks slowly along the line as on a path of light.)

Now you can show her your strength so she can learn from your strength. The light of that strength and trust can really bring warmth.

C.: *Yes.*

(Carla has arrived at the present on her time line, her body erect, eyes straight ahead, breathing deeply and smoothly and smiling broadly.)

R.: I think this is a good place to stop.

(To audience): Thank you for your patience and your support.

Work Of Reimprinting

This demonstration showed more than the technique of reimprinting. It demonstrated some common kinds of impasses and beliefs and how to deal with them. For example, we had some good instances of smoke screens, where smoke screens come from and how they manifest.

Red Herring: The Man

We also had some examples of what could have been a red herring. We could have focused on the man, but he was not really so important in the solution for the system as the mother. Some people might just focus on the relationship between the child and the man, and not the whole system. Also, the problem was not so much caused by a single issue or single belief as much as by a system of relationships.

Turning the Impasse Into a Resource

Notice that the thing that seemed to be an impasse—"It is all around me and I can't escape from it"—now becomes a very powerful resource because now, that strength is all around me the way the problem used to be.

In other words, when that resource is put in place of the pain, or of the gun, the resource is everywhere—in the same way that pain was everywhere, or that *"thing"* was everywhere.

The Molecule Of Identity: The Necessity Of Sorting It Out

This demonstration showed a number of things about beliefs; about how your relationship with the client enters into it, and how a molecule that created the initial problem, the initial impasse, needs to be broken apart and reorganized. But it is not a molecule just of visual, auditory, and kinesthetic representations, but *a molecule of relationships and identity.*

First we address the imprint experience from within, then we get outside of it and clarify each of the positions. Then we want to bring in resources. We still use the same elements, but with a different organization, a different relationship.

I want to draw a parallel with what we were doing in reimprinting and what we were doing with the *"failure into feedback" technique* we went over in the previous section. Instead of just taking the visual, auditory, kinesthetic representations, and putting them into the accessing cues, we took the different identities and sorted them spatially, so nothing was confused in the present.

That is *basically the goal of reimprinting: find the relational molecule.* Get outside of that molecule so we can reorganize it into a new relationship where each person in the system supports the other rather than hurting the other.

Steps Of The Process

1. Find the impasse

First we find the expression of the symptom in the present; we want to find out as much as we can in the present:

where the impasse is; (the expression of the symptom)

what stops you from being able to make a change, or to move on?

2. Create an associated time line

I like making a *physical time line because it helps to organize the elements of the system in the same way* as putting the senses into their accessing cues helps organize them and keep them separate. It often happens, in the mind, that all these incidents from different times collect together into a kind of hologram. Of course, that can sometimes be overwhelming.

It is much easier to deal with all of these things one at a time. Also, a limiting belief that has been established early on starts creating other beliefs, and other beliefs... So *if we can get back to the first belief and shift that one, everything else starts to rearrange itself.*

It is much easier to do that than to try to work with this belief in the present. It will be more like dominos, each knocking the other one down as you grow up.

3. Transderivational Search

So you take the impasse or the expression of the symptom. *You step onto the time line associated,* and you allow yourself to *go back, leaving the incidents associated with the impasse* in the places where they belong on the time line until you get back to the first incident.

This doesn't have to be conscious. You don't even have to be able to visualize to do this. Very often you will find that you are going on this line, and you know that something happened about here. You are not sure what it is, but you know that it was important.

That is fine. You can just mark that spot and keep going. It doesn't always have to be conscious; that is the nice thing about a physical time line. Very often you know physically, even though you don't know consciously.

So you go back until you find the earliest incident. Maybe it is just a feeling that this is the first one. How you know that is not important. *We are not talking about objective reality.* We are talking about something much more important: *subjective reality, which really determines how you act.*

4. Locate a Pre-imprint Perspective

We then want to *take a step to before the imprint occurred.* That is important sometimes.

I found that in a lot of phobias, for instance, people have a "movie" of an incident that runs over and over. It doesn't have a beginning, it doesn't have an end by itself. So you say, "Go to a time before that incident happened, when you were safe, and then find the time after it was over that you were safe."

It is bound on either side by safety, and you know that it ended, and there is even a beginning where you might be able to make some changes that could have prevented the incident. I call this *making a safety sandwich.*

For instance, do you remember when we were finding a place before Carla's imprint happened? She stepped over it, and we went to before any of that happened. So we established a place that came before the time period associated with the imprint.

This "safety sandwich" won't always resolve it, of course, and that is what happened to Carla. She established the time before, but as long as she was on the line the incident could still find her—which is alright.

Since we are after the beliefs formed by the incident, I want to keep the person associated in the imprint experience. That is why we were standing on the line for a while. I want to have *the person verbalize the beliefs, or the generalizations that were formed* by that experience.

Some of Carla's beliefs were:

> *I can't talk about it.*
>
> *I can't know it.*
>
> *I can't escape from it.*

Those were all beliefs that were important for us to know about—not so much the content of what happened but what sort of beliefs the incident created. At this point, we are not trying to fix anything. We just want to find the beliefs.

5. Dissociate the subject from the time line

Then we *dissociate from it,* and at this point we literally *step off the line to the outside* so we are not in it anymore. We are looking at it: *here is an incident, here is before, here is after.*

So I have got a meta-position. I also want to find out what other beliefs there are from this position, because this perspective is different from the associated perspective.

From inside this experience, the belief might have been, "Oh, I am being a good girl, I am giving pleasure."

But from the dissociated position you may think, "That is disgusting and shameful."

The belief here on the line could be different from the belief in the dissociated position.

I can't always understand the whole problem space just from the belief that developed in one perspective; it is the whole system of beliefs. That is why you want to get a number of beliefs. Sometimes the belief out here in the dissociated position can be very resourceful too. I can suddenly realize that I responded with the best resources that I had at that time with the limited view of the world I had then.

6. Positive intention of the impasse

At this stage, you want to *find the positive intention of this impasse.*

Do you remember when we were out here, and I said, "This *"thing"* is a part of you and it has a positive intention"?

From meta-position, I want to find the positive purpose of that impasse: Maybe it has been to protect me, or prevent me from forgetting something important.

In Carla's case it was: "To not be dishonest with myself, and to establish limits."

How to *establish limits* was part of the belief issue that was going on here. Each person in the imprint relationship needed to have limits.

The child needs to know if it is alright to be creative, and explore inside limits.

The mother needs to be able to set limits on the behavior of people that she cares about.

The man has to realize his own limits: what is the limit of playing?

It was all about *where the appropriate limits are; how does a person set criteria to know how far to go within a particular system and still remain ecological?*

Also notice that from out here, when we dissociate and go to a meta-position, we want to identify *any of the significant others that were in the experience, and make sure we understand the intention of each of those people.*

In a way none of them really had an evil or malicious intention; to want pleasure is not an evil intention.

People deserve pleasure. The question is where the limits are, in order to make having pleasure ecological.

I don't think that anybody in Carla's system was a bad person. But they obviously needed additional resources.

7. Needed resources

Now the question is to find *what the resources are, and at what level the different individuals needed them and didn't have them.*

These levels are important because sometimes you ask, "What did you need?" and get the answer, "I needed not to be there, I needed to be somewhere else."

That is an *environmental resource*, and that is certainly valid. But it is not all you would need. You may need a *behavioral resource* to accomplish that change in environment.

"Which behavioral resource would you have needed to be able to do something that would have enabled you to be somewhere else? What would you have needed to get to a different environment?"

Of course, in order to do things behaviorally, you have to have inner knowledge. You may need to have a broader perspective. You *need capabilities* that maybe you didn't have, or your parents didn't have, or whoever else was involved did not have.

Sometimes people say that *they just needed to either run away or kill that person.* That is of course just *a behavior*

BOOK LIST

Meta Publications Inc.
P. O. Box 565, Cupertino, CA 95015
(415) 965-0954

Quantity

_____ **Beyond Selling** $19.95
Dan S. Bagley & Edward J. Reese (hardcover)

_____ **Time Line Therapy** $22.95
Tad James & Wyatt Woodsmall (hardcover)

_____ **The Magic of Rapport** $12.95
Jerry Richardson (hardcover)

_____ **An Insider's Guide To Submodalities** $12.95
Richard Bandler & Will MacDonald (paper)

_____ **Thinking About Thinking** $10.95
Joseph Yeager (paper)

_____ **The Master Moves** $14.95
Moshe Feldenkrais (hardcover)

_____ **Magic in Action** $14.95
Richard Bandler (hardcover)

_____ **Roots of Neuro-Linguistic Programming** $22.00
Robert Dilts (hardcover)

_____ **Applications of Neuro-Linguistic Programming** $22.00
Robert Dilts (hardcover)

_____ **Meta-Cation: Prescriptions for Some
Ailing Educational Processes** $12.00
Sid Jacobson (hardcover)

_____ **Meta-Cation: Volume II** $12.00
Sid Jacobson (hardcover)

_____ **Meta-Cation: Volume III** $12.00
Sid Jacobson (hardcover)

_____ **Phoenix—Therapeutic Patterns of
Milton H. Erickson** $14.00
D. Gordon & M. Myers-Anderson (hardcover)

_____ **Neuro-Linguistic Programming** $24.00
Dilts, Grinder, Bandler et al Limited Edition (hardcover)

_____ **The Elusive Obvious** $20.00
Moshe Feldenkrais (deluxe edition)

_____ **Patterns of Hypnotic Techniques of
Milton H. Erickson, M.D. - Volume I** $10.95
Bandler and Grinder (paper)

(See other side for more books and order form.)

_____ **Patterns of Hypnotic Techniques of Milton H. Erickson, M.D. - Volume II** $17.95
Bandler, DeLozier, Grinder (hardcover)

_____ **Provocative Therapy** $12.95
Farrelly & Brandsma (hardcover)

_____ **The Structure of Magic, Volume I** $10.95
Bandler and Grinder (paper)

_____ **The Structure of Magic, Volume II** $10.95
Bandler and Grinder (paper)

_____ **Practical Magic** $12.95
Stephen R. Lankton (hardcover)

_____ **Therapeutic Metaphors** $12.95
David Gordon (hardcover)

ORDER FORM

FOLD AND MAIL THIS CARD WITH YOUR CHECK TO:

Meta Publications Inc.
P. O. Box 565, Cupertino, CA 95015
(415) 965-0954

Please send me copies of the books ordered

Subtotal   _____

Tax (add 7% for California residents)   _____

Freight & Handling   2.00

TOTAL AMOUNT ENCLOSED   _____

Name _____

Address _____

City _____ State _____ Zip _____

Charge to my credit card: Exp. Date

☐ Visa # _____ _____

☐ MasterCard # _____ _____

Phone (   ) _____

Signature _____
(Credit Card Only)

that is not always the choice that is the most appropriate or ecological for the whole system.

When you are at the level of behavior, it is important that there is a number of choices. You want to have a number of possibilities that would actually give you more appropriate choices. *So the capability to create other choices is more general than specific behaviors.*

I might say, "My mother needed to say something to that person." It is a behavior to say something. But *what is the capability that is needed to know what to say?* I might need some communication skills. I might need some good N.L.P. ideas here.

"My mother would be great if she had N.L.P. strategies."

In order to be capable of facing that situation and saying what needs to be said, I may need a resource at the belief level, or perhaps even at the identity level.

In a sense, I think that was where the strength came from in Carla's case: trust, belief in myself, feeling my identity, setting limits. Having an identity and treating the others as identities, I think, was one of the very interesting things about what happened within Carla's system.

When the mother said to the man, "I acknowledge you, I love you, but I am going to do anything in my power to protect my daughter and you ought to know that."

To me *that is true love.* That is not dependency or co-dependency, that is an acknowledgement.

When people can do that with one another, when one person can express a pure identity without judgement, without hatred, then it is a moment of intensity between the two filled with respect and acknowledgement, not judgement of bad or good. That is what brought peace to the man as well as change in his behavior.

Again, at this stage we find *which resources* are needed. And you might need resources at all levels. I don't think that in all situations you will need to go up all the levels. I think you can see that Carla's imprint was obviously a big situation, bigger than what you may find in many lives. But regardless of the content, hers were issues that everybody has to face in their lives at one point—not hiding from themselves or reality or their own weaknesses.

If somebody says, "I just needed to *know* this and that," or "My mother needed to have such and such knowledge," that is, of course, a capability. Sometimes that new capability will be all that is needed. Sometimes, even though some people might have the belief and the identity resources already, they just don't have the information. Sometimes people have the information, but they are denying it because they don't have the belief in themselves.

So what is important when you are finding the needed resources is that you ask, "At which level(s) is the resource necessary?" And find the needed resources for each perceptual position.

The ability to take multiple perceptual positions is important in areas other than therapy. If you are a leader in a business and you have no idea of what your employees feel, think, or believe, you won't be a very good manager because you have no idea what it is like to be inside their shoes.

True adults know what it is like to be a parent and to be a child. They do not view reality just from one position or the other.

In a sense, this is what we are talking about here: *There are parts of me that are both the adult as well as the child.*

When I go up here in a third position (the meta-position out of the system and the time line), *I go to a position in which my identity is not invested in either of the individuals involved, and I can become aware of the relationship.*

After we identify the needed resource and what level it is on, *then we want to access that resource in the person, in the subject.*

It doesn't matter if the mother never had it. It doesn't matter if the child didn't have it at that time. What is important is that the resource exists, and the subject has access to it in the present and can feel it. Even if it was only for a moment in your life, you can grab it, and if you put it in at the imprint experience, it will start to make more of itself; it will start to grow like a mustard seed.

The point is not to fool the subjects about the reality of what happened.

They can always remember what did actually happen. But rather than having this memory be a scar, so whenever you think about it you regress back into confusion and helplessness, you bring the solution *into* the memory. So not only can you remember what really happened, but you remember the solution as well. *And the solution is real.*

The important thing to remember about personal history is that *you are not the content of the experiences that happened to you. You are your resources.* That is the reality of life; not, "I have to be like my past was."

The reality is that I am the beliefs and the capabilities and the behaviors that I learned from my personal history.

So instead of repeating my mistakes I am learning from them. *Carla's memory can give her strength and peace* as much as confusion and denial.

8. Transfer the resource

So, once we anchor this needed resource in the place on the time line where the subject can really experience the resource fully, we want to bring it into the imprint experience, and watch it change from the resource spot on the time line. One method I often use to accomplish this transfer of resources is to have the subject imagine the resource as a particular color and quality of light. Then imagine sending that light back through time to the person in the system who needed it.

One reason for doing this from a distance is that, if there is a problem with it, we can always add another resource before the subject associates back into the imprint.

We test the resources when the person is still dissociated from the imprint, and not associated with it on his time line.

We watch how the relationships within that system will change. We want to first see them from the outside. Once I have done this I will know that the new resources are both effective and ecological.

9. Associate into the functional relationship.

Then the subject needs to *experience the change fully from the associated position. This is why you take the resource and have the subject step into the significant others, and notice what it is like from inside their perceptual positions.*

There were a number of individuals in Carla's situation; we could have taken resources to other people as well. The basic question is, "What is needed to achieve the critical mass that will change the system?" For Carla the most critical element was the mother. If she changed, everything else evolved as well.

We could have gone back more times and given more resources to the child or to the other adults and repeat this again and again until we were done with everybody. Then each member of the system would have become part of the solution as well. For instance, I think it is important to take resources to the man and literally go through from his perspective, because Carla could learn a lot from that.

It is often valuable to take a resource to the aggressor for two reasons: first, if the child knows what resource that person needs, she can prevent that kind of situation from happening in the future because she will be able to recognize somebody that has what is needed to act in an appropriate way, or doesn't have it. If a child goes through life thinking that all men are bad, she will never learn what the distinctions are between a person who has resources and a person who does not have them.

If I can put the resource in, see it, hear it, and feel it; then I can sense if it is there or not in somebody when I am around them.

The second reason is that if it is not there in somebody in reality, perhaps it can be drawn out of him, or brought to him, so he can change. But until someone has the knowledge to make the distinction he will always be a victim of chance.

10. Returning to the Present.

After we step back into the imprint, we want to see *how that resource changes or affects each related situation coming after the imprint experience.* So we have the subject walk on his time line towards the present to see if these later experiences support the learnings from the new resources in a kind of "domino effect." As Carla said to me after the process, when you make that much change you can get pretty fatigued, and *that is why you need to let things have a chance to change.* So sometimes it is a good idea to stop and rest before going to the next step.

The important thing about reimprinting is that its purpose is to find the role model, to find the imprint, the personal "archetype." Then *pace* and *lead that role model* instead of trying to get rid of it, deny it, or fight it. Acknowledge it and lead it.

I think that, in some sense, in Carla's metaphor of the gun, everybody was pointing the gun at their own heads in that system.

The child enjoyed the situation, then felt ashamed. The mother ignored it, then felt guilty and ashamed. The man couldn't help it, and I am sure at one point he started to point the gun at his own head as well.

Everybody was doing the same thing: ignore the problem in the system until it was too late to do something about it, then feel guilty and ashamed.

This same kind of dysfunctional pattern can happen in businesses and social systems as well. There is an interesting book called *The Addictive Organization* in which the authors claim that addictions start around anything that people feel that they have to lie about.

Recognizing the need for a strong identity makes a whole different situation. It not only resolves this memory but creates a positive reference. So now, and in the future, if Carla starts getting that feeling: "I don't know if I should face this or handle that," she will know the place she needs to operate from inside herself, and what resources she needs: strength and peace to acknowledge, communicate and set appropriate limits.

SUMMARY OF Reimprinting Technique

An *imprint* is a significant experience or sequence of experiences from the past in which a person formed a belief or cluster of beliefs.

An imprint experience also often involves the *unconscious role-modeling* of significant others.

The purpose of reimprinting is to find the resources necessary to change the beliefs and update the role models that were formed; not simply to resolve the emotional issues as in the N.L.P. technique of *change personal history.*

1. Identify the specific symptoms (which may be feelings, words, or images) associated with the impasse. Most people want to avoid the symptoms because they are uncomfortable. But it is important to remember that avoiding them won't resolve the limitation.

Have the subject focus on the symptoms, *step* onto *the* time line (facing the future) and walk slowly backwards until he reaches the earliest experience of the feeling and/or symptoms associated with the impasse.

Keeping the subject in the associated/regressed state, have him verbalize the generalizations or beliefs that were formed from the experience.

2. Have the subject take a step backwards to a time before the initial imprint experience. Then have the subject step off the time line and return to the present and look back at the imprint experience from "meta-position."

Ask the subject to notice the effect that earlier experience has had on his life. Also have the subject verbalize any other generalizations or beliefs that were formed as a result of the imprint experience. (Beliefs are often formed "after the fact.")

3. Find the positive intent or the secondary gain of the symptoms or responses formed at the imprint experience. Also identify any significant others involved in the imprint. The symptoms may actually come from the role modeling of significant others. Find the positive intention of their behavior

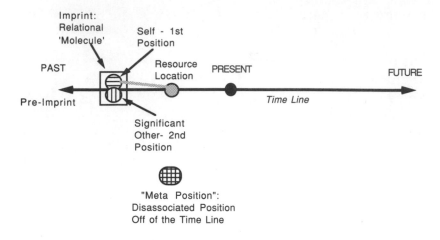

Figure 15. Map of Re-Imprinting Technique

as well. This may be done by associating into the significant other in the experience and viewing it from his point of view.

4. For *each* of the people involved in the imprint experience:

    a. Identify the *resources* or choices that the person needed back then, and did not have, but that *the subject does have available now.* Remember that you need not limit yourself to the capabilities that the subject or the significant others had at that time. So long as the subject (not the significant others) has those resources available now, you may use them to help change that experience. Have the subject step onto his time line at the location where he most strongly experienced having that resource and anchor it. [Make sure the resource is at the appropriate logical level.]

    b. 'Transmit' the resource to the significant other. This may be accomplished by imagining the resource as a beam of light that can be shined back across the time line and inside of the other person. Notice how this resource changes the dynamics of the whole system. Adjust or add to the resource if necessary.

c. Holding the resource anchor, have the subject step off the time line, walk back to the imprint experience, step into the position of the person who needed the resource, and relive the imprint experience from that person's point of view, incorporating the needed resource.

d. Ask the subject to step off the time line, out of the imprint experience, and update or modify the generalizations he would now choose to make from the experience.

Repeat this procedure for each of the significant people involved in the imprint experience.

5. Ask the subject to identify the most important resource or belief that he would have needed from his own point of view. Anchor that resource and take it back to the location on the time line before the imprint occurred. Have the subject take the resource into his younger self and walk all the way up the time line to the present, experiencing the changes made by the reimprinting.

Try this process for yourself. It is often important to acknowledge and update significant relationships from the past.

For example, when I was working with my mother on her cancer, an interesting issue arose at one point. Her older sister and her mother had both died of breast cancer. Some people have this kind of funny sense that in order to be loyal, in order to keep their allegiance, their affiliation with their family, they have to follow the family pattern. It is kind of like: "Who am I to be any better than those people who are my models, my mentors?"

Furthermore, if they transcended the family pattern they have no role models; they are on their own.

I think that sometimes people might prefer to die rather than face the unknown. Obviously, this is not a situation that you can resolve by using submodalities to put it out of your mind. So I asked my mother to go to meta-position, and I said, "Instead of just looking to the past to see your sister and your mother, in order to know your identity and how you should be, look for a moment to the future and see your daughter, who is looking at you to see how she should be." That helped to put the issue in a broader perspective.

It was a very powerful experience for her and one that she returns to often to make decisions.

I find the same kind of imprinting issues sometimes happening to people in business situations. Imagine someone from a working-class family who reaches a point of success in his work and suddenly he is going to be promoted to a white-collar position. You might have quite a crisis, because he is breaking his family pattern, his cultural identity.

Success can create as much crisis as failure.

When this working-class person started his job maybe he looked at successful people and said, "They don't know what anything is about, they are a bunch of jerks."

Imagine his surprise when he suddenly finds himself being one of those persons!

These kinds of relational issues enter our lives in many, many different ways. I think that it is important to realize the power of and sometimes the need to update those role models, so they become supportive; because someday you will step into one of those roles.

Exercise

Now lay out your own time line. Maybe in following the demonstration you already have some ideas of where some of the issues are for you. And certainly your unconscious mind does.

Take whatever *struggle, impasse, or symptoms you have in the present.* Step on the line, *find the initial imprint and identity, and the beliefs you built from it. Then go back before the imprint,* step off the line, and look at the key relationships in the imprint. *Find the positive intention and the needed resources of each significant person in the system.*

Even though the situation may seem complex, I think that if you can at least find one significant other person, bring them a resource, and update the system, this will be a powerful exercise for you. Sometimes you need to do one and let it integrate for a while. Very often that will start everything else happening anyway. That may be all that is needed. Any questions?

Q.: *When you say that you are going back into the past, letting the unconscious speak, is there still one moment when you identify precisely something, and there is a picture?*

R.: When I am doing this, I don't have to have a picture at all. Remember that with Carla we didn't start having any pictures before stepping off the line. Sometimes you will get no picture when you are associated in the imprint experience, but when you get out, then you start getting the images. It doesn't have to be objectively correct, either. You may not know if what you see is really what happened, or whether the memory is from so long ago that it is all distorted. What is important to me is the distortion anyway, not the reality.

Q.: *But there is a picture?*

R.: Often, yes. A person might say, "I don't see a clear picture, but I just sense or know that was what was happening..."

It doesn't have to be a clear picture, as long as you can tell the relationships that were involved.

After The Exercise

R.: Questions, comments, experiences to be shared?

Q.: *At one point, as the person was in meta-position, I had the impression that the resource was inefficient, but the subject said it was good enough. So, just to make sure, I had the person go back on her time line; as she faced her experience, she said: "It is inefficient." I had to get her out in order to go on.*

R.: That is very nice. This is using your experience as feedback, as opposed to failure. What is nice is that you have a way of immediately getting back out to add the resource. Sometimes you need to combine two or three resources.

This is when *the fish in the dreams* enters the picture. The subject might have his own fish in his dreams. From a dissociated position he says, "Oh, I discovered the solution," but when he associates back into the imprint, he discovers it is not enough. So that's why you say, "Let's check to make sure that is not just a fish in a dream."

Again, I really want to acknowledge the fact that if you don't get it right immediately it means nothing, because you have a context where you can go and get more resources. That is a discovery, an insight, a feedback, and a resource to both the programmer and the subject. That is a success.

Beliefs And Logical Levels

Q.: *Can a belief system or a sequence of beliefs be bound or provoked by a previous belief?*

R.: Yes.

Q.: *In this case the belief went back to a very young age and was: "I have no right to exist." In such a belief, what are the relationships with identity?*

R.: This kind of belief is obviously about identity. In fact, these are the kinds of basic beliefs that form identity.

If I start with an early belief that *I don't belong,* I will start to find evidence of it. If I get a spanking from my parents, I will say that is a proof. And if they tell me something nice, *"they are just lying to me, fooling me."* So starting with that kind of belief sets a frame that determines how everything afterwards gets interpreted.

If I start with the belief that *"I do belong,"* then if they say something nice they are reinforcing it. If I get punished, *"I will wonder why they are doing that. There must be something I have to learn from this."* It is not taken as a statement about my identity, but about behavior.

Imprints And Developmental Sequence

That kind of belief is common, in a way. There is a certain time when people will build those beliefs. In the work I was doing with Timothy Leary, we were in fact working with a developmental model.

It said that certain types of imprints had to do with certain issues that you could trace to a certain developmental sequence. The sequence is somewhat related to Maslow's hierarchy of needs, but it has some important differences.

The first stage involves *imprints at the level of biological intelligence,* which has to do with survival. "Can I survive?" As a child the first thing you need to figure out is how to manage your basic biological functioning. Even the simplest organism has to learn to survive.

The next stage involves *emotional imprints: With whom do I belong? Where are my bonds? What is my territory?*

The next stage involves the development of *intellectual imprints: Am I smart? Can I think? Am I dextrous?* This stage has to do with capabilities, in a way. It involves the development of abilities to understand symbols and process them efficiently.

The next stage involves *social imprints: What is my role in relationship to others?*

After that you enter a stage in which you develop an *aesthetic imprint.* That is when you start to begin to be aware of things for what they are, and are finally able to perceive beauty and forms: *What is beautiful? What is pleasurable?*

Finally there is a stage in which you develop imprints on a *meta level,* what you might call *spiritual* or *identity level imprints,* where you start turning back your awareness onto all of the previous stages. *What makes me the way I am? In what ways can I evolve myself?*

Analogy With a Company

I think that cultures and businesses go through the same stages.

First, *can I survive?* Then, *where's my territory? Where do I belong? Then I begin to get smarter, to learn how to deal with the market and with other companies.* Then *I become more socially aware.* The company will finally reach a level of aesthetic awareness where it will really get concerned with the quality of the product—not necessarily because that will help it to survive but because of the beauty of the product itself.

It then begins to evaluate itself, to expand and evolve its own inner structure.

If there is a negative imprint in one of these stages it makes it difficult to go to the next level. The chain is no stronger than its weakest link. And if pressure is exerted onto the system it will often regress back to this particular stage, because it has unfinished business at this stage, or is missing a resource that should have been learned or developed at that stage.

Q.: *Can you give a **rough idea of critical ages for these stages of imprints?***

R.: In general, I think that *very small children are in the survival stage.* But it is *rather early on that they will start bonding.*

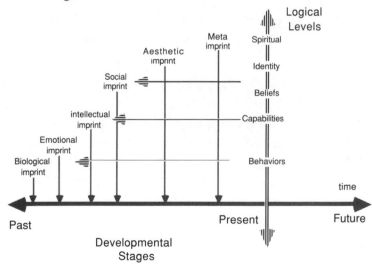

Figure 16. Imprints and Developmental Stages of Intelligence

First, you *bond* with the mother, then you start bonding with members of the larger system, i.e., father, brothers, etc. People often start picking up intellectual stage imprints *in primary school.* "Am I smart in comparison to the other children?" and so on.

And then you get to *early teens,* young adolescents. *Adolescents get very concerned about their social image.* They are very concerned about social perception. *Very often aesthetic imprints come around college level.* And following that, the meta-level.

This is very general. Depending upon cultural and family systems, and the environment, people might be forced into some imprint experiences earlier.

Q.: *When you go back to such an experience, you go back to one belief like, "I have no right to exist," and you take the resource from the person in meta and inject it in each one of the characters of the situation and, when the person feels it is alright to come back to the present you have them relive events one after the other; I am wondering if it changes the belief system linked to the first belief?*

R.: The kind of belief that you are talking about is what I call a *CORE BELIEF.* A core belief is a very general and basic belief that will influence anything that comes after it. *"If I don't belong here, who cares how smart I am?" "If I don't belong here, why would I want to have a social role?"* That is going to affect everything else that comes after.

Q.: *I did the exercise as subject and was struck by the fact that when all my past was before me, I was unable to experience it fully. I had to turn my back on the future to find the joy and pleasure I had before.*

R.: Were you able to change the imprint so that you could feel resourceful when you were looking at the future from that position?

Q.: *All this was before being in meta-position.*

R.: Notice how perspective changes your whole experience of something. I can reaccess the same feelings if I relive the event that created those feelings. But if I am looking at the same event from a meta-position off of the time line, I perceive them differently and they have a different impact.

If I perceive the same events on the time line, but from a point before or after them in time, the content of the events is the same, but the feelings are different. The changes come from my position with respect to the events. That is a large part of what this process is about.

Meta-Programs and Positions on the Time Line

In a way, the reimprinting context provides you with a means to change meta-program patterns and sorting styles. For instance, you can easily influence a person to be *in time* or *through time, away from* or *toward,* or sort by *the present to the past* or *the past to the future,* or *the present to the future.* You can have the person sort by *self,* by *others,* by *context.*

What you have with this particular model is a set of dimensions that creates a context for change. The change comes from the intersection of perspective levels and time frames in this context.

So we have time on a first axis. We also have logical levels: identity, beliefs, capabilities, behaviors, and environment on a second axis, and perceptual position on a third axis—self, other, meta-position, which are all involved in meta-programs.

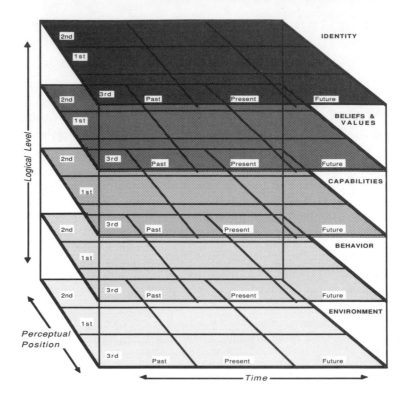

Figure 17. Contextual Workspace for Meta Programs

So what I have inside of this structure is a gestalt, a contextual space for my life that gives me a place to go to find the resources that I need. The interaction of all those dimensions helps to create the change.

Where I physically stand in this contextual space will actually shift the meta-program that I am operating from at the time.

Q.: *I believe what you have just said answers a question that I had.* **Do these traumatic experiences crystalize some meta-program patterns?**

R.: Yes; a habitual meta-program pattern forms because maybe at this earlier time I didn't know the other positions to go to. Maybe it forms because that was the first time that I ever had that meta-program perception. It becomes crystalized, as you said. It becomes like a piece of sand in an oyster; the rest of the pearl begins to form around that imprint until we get back inside the layers surrounding that grain of sand. Then we can shift that sand a little and grow an even more beautiful and exquisite pearl.

With this process we work to resolve belief issues relating to the past in order to clear personal history and help us deal better with relationships to others. Once we have made peace with others and peace with our past, then it is time to make peace with ourselves and face the future. This is where we will head next.

To conclude our work with reimprinting, *let's sum up all the important points.*

The Time Line and the Redecision Process

Somebody asked what I do with a person who has the belief, "I am a fat person."

That is a core belief about identity.

> *So how do I change such a core belief? How do I get the person ready to take on a new identity?*

Well, first I want to find the core belief, the grain of sand that started shaping that identity. I want to go back to where the person first made that decision. Maybe I will even find that there are some other core beliefs before that.

Then I want to step out and find the circumstances in which the person made those decisions.

Sometimes you will find that the person's mother was obese: "And I have to be like my mother."

Sometimes you will find that the mother was thin: "I am not going to be like my mother at all."

Sometimes it is: "Nobody takes care of me so I have to feed myself."

I want to find what belief and situation led to that decision about his identity. We then bring new resources to that past situation, and have the person realize, "This is a decision that I made. Is that the most appropriate decision? Is that what all of these things added up to? Or did I only come to that decision because of the limited perspective and resources that I had then?"

Then I take the new decision all the way to the present. We break up the old molecule, but we need to put these elements back together in a way that will draw the person appropriately and ecologically to the future.

Sometimes I need to build a new capability to build a new belief. And sometimes it is not until I free the person from the old belief that the person is even ready to accept and learn the new capability.

Imaginary Fleas

I will give you an example. David Gordon and I were working with a woman many years ago who had an obsession. She believed that bugs got on her. She called them real imaginary fleas; imaginary because nobody else accepted that they were real. But they were real because when they got on her, she felt it. She couldn't ignore it. They gave her the terrible feeling that she was being invaded.

She had to do something to protect herself from them. So she had seventy two different pairs of gloves: for driving her car, putting on her clothes, etc. She always bought clothes that were longer than her arms. She would scrub and scrub her skin so it was red all the time. She was really in a rather stuck situation.

As the fleas were imaginary, that gave them some interesting options. For example, everybody had fleas—especially her parents. She loved her parents dearly, of course, but as they had the most fleas, she couldn't spend much time with them. And as the fleas were imaginary they could even come through the telephone, so when her parents called, fleas would flow from the receiver. That was her belief.

Of course, lots of people tried to convince her it was all crazy. David and I did a number of things to get rapport with her, to find out about her sub-modalities and strategies, but the thing that really put this belief over the threshold was when I started pacing her belief system. I said, "Alright, there are these fleas. But it seems to me that you have been operating *away from* them all your life. You have been trying to get rid of the fleas; you have always tried to make them go away. Maybe that's an ineffective way to deal with them. Has anybody ever treated your real imaginary *allergy* to the real imaginary fleas?

"Because to me it matches all the symptoms of an allergy. Some people have an allergy to pollen in the air; they can't see pollen but it gets in their noses and they feel bad. They don't always have to hide from the pollen or make it go away. There are medicines that treat the immune system to reduce the allergy symptoms."

Then I pulled out a bottle of PLACEBOS and explained, "These are real imaginary pills. They are imaginary because they don't have any real drugs in them, but they are real because they will cure your allergy and change your feeling."

Since we knew all about the sub-modalities of her belief strategy, I started to describe how they would work, how she would feel, and how it would be different according to her critical sub-modalities. Of course she couldn't find any holes in this logic. But the most interesting thing was that when she came back the next week she was really frightened. The reason was because those real imaginary pills had worked.

She sat down and said, "How will I know what kind of clothes to buy? How will I know how to interact with my parents? How will I know who to let touch me? How will I know what to do or where to go in the world around me?"

You must realize that if we couldn't have helped her build the strategies to fill that hole, she might have had to go back to the obsession for ecological reasons. "Here I am, left with the unknown."

She was saying that this belief had substituted for many of her decision-making capabilities. This was an important feedback; it was certainly not a problem. So she was finally ready to hear what a strategy for making a decision is. We went back through and helped her build all these capabilities.

We explored what kind of criteria she should use for answering the "how will I know" questions she brought up and how to find the evidence of these criteria.

We also took some decision-making resources that she had developed and brought them back to the little girl who decided to build these fleas to begin with, because she had this obsession for over fifteen years.

The point is that beliefs, capabilities, and all of the levels join together to make up the total system of a person.

Love

As we bring this exploration of our relationships to others to an end, I think there is a resource and issue that I would like to leave you with: Love. Certainly our lives are shaped by love and those we do love. Today we perhaps got a further insight into what it means to "love another as ourselves."

I think there are different types of love. Often we initially start with *a love that is based around behavior.* Maybe that is a love built around sexuality or mutual caring—somebody helps me survive, I help them survive.

Then we begin perhaps *to love somebody for what they think,* how they are, what they know. Instead of being attracted to somebody because of their bodies, or what kind of car they have or how much money they make, we begin to care about somebody *because of their mind.*

A deeper level of love begins when you start sharing beliefs and values. Then there is a level *when you start sharing an identity.*

You have a friendship or a relationship, not because of what somebody believes or what they have, but because of what they are.

There even comes the time when we jump to a type of love that is above all that: a spiritual type of love. I think this is both important in the development of the relationship and the ending of the relationships.

In some sense, if you have a relationship at a spiritual level, it is never over. Anyone who has experienced the death of somebody that they loved has reached that stage when you can no longer directly experience that person's identity, behavior, belief, etc. The connection needs to move to this spiritual level.

I have seen people who, at a loved one's death or the end of a relationship, take on that person's behaviors. That is sometimes a very useful and important part of whatever ritual you might want to have at the ending of a relationship.

When that person is present they fulfill that part of the system. But when they are no longer there, you have to start providing both capabilities yourself. Sometimes certain beliefs and values intensify. Sometimes, as many of you may discover from the reimprinting process you take on aspects of the identities of these significant others.

I think that is a process that is important for going through what is called grief—to be able to integrate all those levels of relationship.

A few years ago my father had a stroke. It wasn't expected. He was only fifty-seven. He had a massive stroke and was not supposed to survive more than a few hours. So my family rushed to the hospital to be with him.

We began to do all the things that we could do to help him heal and keep him alive. From the experience that I had with my mother and with other health issues, I wanted to try everything within my power that I could.

He survived that day and began to survive other days. And yet, when you have a stroke, the situation actually gets worse over time because the brain swells and the skull doesn't expand, so it starts squeezing your brain out of the bottom of your skull. This really messes up all your vital functions: body temperature, breathing, blood pressure, and heart rate. It is an interesting paradox, because in trying to heal itself, your body is actually harming itself. The brain that is organizing all this is the part that is damaged.

My Dad's situation was getting worse, and the doctors were saying he was in a coma and couldn't hear us anymore. Of course we had a lot of hope and were trying to do anything we could. We also believed that he could still hear us. However, his body was getting weaker and weaker. He lost a quarter of his body weight. He was blinded because of the stroke. He couldn't move the right side of his body at all and couldn't control the left side.

Of course, it was difficult for me to see my father, who had always been strong and in control, withering away to nothing.

On the fifth and sixth days things were really bad. It was as if we had tried to run together as hard as we could and had fallen face down into the mud. And we dragged ourselves up and gave it everything we had again, only to fall again and again and again.

My mother and sister and I were in with my father, asking him for some kind of sign that he was still there. We were all wanting to keep him alive.

All of a sudden this person that couldn't urinate on his own, blind, his body withered to nothing, barely able to control any of his own functions, lifted up his left hand and grabbed my head, pulled my ear to his mouth, and made a noise that I thought to be "Hi," but it was "Good-bye." Then he began to reach around with his hand in his blindness and he found my sister's hand, put it on top of his hand, found my mother's hand and put it on top of my sister's hand, and found my hand, put it on top of my mother's hand, and put his other hand on top of all of our hands. That was the last conscious act that he made. I have never seen anything more beautiful.

That night my mother had a dream in which she saw my father. He was sixteen years old again, which is how old he was when they fell in love.

In her dream, she could see that he was going away, and of course she didn't want him to go. She wanted him to stay or go with him. First she was angry, then sad.

But she said that he looked so happy about where he was going (being sixteen again) that she couldn't make him stay.

Then he turned to her and said that where he was going she couldn't follow him; it wasn't her time to go yet. It may seem as if it would be a long time before she saw him again, but in a larger scope of time it would be hardly any time at all. When they were together again, it would be forever.

This is a positive imprint for me. When I think about my last act of life, if my body was completely broken and in pain, practically useless—certainly my father had had every right to be completely self-consumed—if I could have that presence of mind to integrate, to finish all of the business that way, if I could use everything I have learned in N.L.P. to be able to do something like that at the end of my physical existence, then it would make my life and learnings worth it.

That's what I would like to get out of N.L.P.

When the time comes—when your whole reality is changing and there is nothing that you can do, and what you never dreamed could happen is happening—then "the only thing you can do is to be impeccable in yourself," as Carlos Castaneda's Don Juan would say.

Meditation On Love

The bond of love is never broken. It just shifts to different levels.

I would like you to close your eyes for a moment and think about some person that you care about but are not always with. It doesn't have to be somebody who is dying or who has passed on. It can be somebody that you have not been together with for a long period of time.

I would like you to notice how you think about that person. Where do you see that person in your mind? What do you hear in your mind? Is it a clear picture? Is it distant? Is it bright?

Then think of either a friend or an object; perhaps something from your past. Even though this person or this thing is no longer with you, you feel as though it is always there with you. It could be a toy that you had; when you remember it you treasure it without sadness. It could be a friend that you always feel that you are with, no matter where you are.

I would like you to notice how you visualize or hear this object, or this person, in your mind so that they can be with you all the time.

Take the memory of the person that you care about but can't be with, and change the qualities of that memory so that they match qualities of the memory of the person or the object that you feel always to be with you. Maybe you bring the image closer. Maybe instead of seeing it behind you or to your left, the location of that image is in your heart. Maybe there is a certain quality of color, or brightness, that makes it seem closer or more present. Maybe there is a particular quality of voice, tone, tempo, or depth.

As you continue to allow that memory of that person to find its place in your mind, in your values and beliefs, in your identity, remember for a moment a feeling of love, of pure love, a love that has no boundaries, it has no quantity, that kind of love that is neither giving nor taking, but just *is*.

Notice where that love comes from. Does it come from somewhere deeply inside you? Is it from within your heart? Or is it all around you?

Begin to visualize that love as a pure, shining light. Let it brighten and shine within and around you. Then take that light. Make it into a shining silvery thread. And tie that thread from your heart to the heart of the person you care about—knowing that this thread of light can connect your heart to their hearts, no matter where they are, how far away, in which time.

It is a thread that you can take to any number of people, a thread that never breaks, a thread that never runs out of light. So as you see yourself sitting here you can see your heart connect with as many threads as those around you that you meet.

Feel the thread coming through now. Then the light of the thread begins to expand and glow, so it fills all the space around you. Know that it is a light that can fill the universe with its brightness.

Feel yourself in this room. Most important, make sure that you can feel that love for yourself. For a moment, feel your own heart as it beats within you.

Know also that you are a complete person, a complete being. Know that you can be an identity, you can be an individual. Feel your own individuality, your uniqueness. Perhaps tonight you might find or notice how those threads have been attached by others to your heart.

Just for a moment, BE in this room, so that your awareness is around nothing else; just be. Allow yourself to sense as fully as possible that being, the sounds, your body, the air and light around you, the air that fills your lungs, brings oxygen and life to all your body. And become aware of the other people around you, other beings, the individuals, special people. As your eyes open and sense the light that fills the room, bring that being completely here.

CHAPTER IV

Integrating Conflicting Beliefs

In this section we are going to work on the integration of conflicting beliefs, and explore how we put together certain parts of our identities or belief systems to work together in such a way that they support one another.

One of my favorite metaphors for the process of belief change comes from a parable of Jesus, where he talks about the sower and the seed.

He says that the sower sows the seed in various places. The seed has the miracle of identity already within it and is able to provide its own path of growth. The sower or the gardener doesn't have to make the seed grow. The seed contains within it the magic of life.

But the sower has to prepare the context. If the sower sows the seed on ground that has no depth, according to the parable, birds snatch the seed away. If the seed falls on rocky ground then the roots grow quickly at first, but when the sun gets hot they are not able to achieve depth because of the rocks, and the plant withers.

If the seed falls on ground with weeds, the roots grow but then get strangled by the weeds as they compete for the same space. It is only when the seeds fall on fertile, deep ground that they are able to grow and bear fruit.

This is a good metaphor for what it means **to develop a new belief or identity.**

A person who has a serious illness can say, "I believe that I can get well."

But often that belief has no ground, no depth. They are just words to the person, just an empty hope. If there are no rich representations, if the person has no inner map of what it would be like visually, auditorily, and kinesthetically to recover and feel good, then there isn't ground with enough depth for this belief to grow.

Then if somebody comes and says, "Oh, that is foolish, of course you can't get well, face the facts: your situation is hopeless."

That is just like the bird that comes and plucks the seed, the belief, from shallow earth. The person is crushed and admits he is doubtful and uncertain.

If the seed has fallen on rocky ground, full of limiting imprints from the past, then even if there is some representation, some part of the person that can accept the belief, the roots of the belief run into some resistance. The roots can grow to a certain degree, but maybe there are those old molecules, those rocks from the past, which keep the roots of this new identity from growing all the way through the richness of the person's life experiences.

When it comes under pressure from the difficulties that are often involved in changing, the new belief begins to wither. There is that old molecule, this old rock from the past that keeps the belief from really taking full root.

Sometimes, if the seed has fallen with other seeds, they begin to compete for whose identity will truly fill the garden. One or the other is going to grow and take the nutrition in the rich soil away from the other. Then you have conflicting identities: two trying to live in the same place.

We have learned, in the past two chapters, ways of building a soil of capabilities, of breaking up those rocks of old beliefs so that they can become soil for growing.

Congruency at the Identity Level

In this chapter, we want to make sure that we are congruent at the identity level as well as at the belief level, so we are not trying to have two different parts that are taking up the same space.

We often find that after a person has cleared her personal history, she is still left with the part of her identity that has developed from those past beliefs. Even though those old rocks or scars are no longer there, she still needs to integrate that part of herself that has grown from the imprint into her whole identity.

For example, I once worked with a woman who had been labeled schizophrenic. She had been hospitalized several times and was quite traumatized by the experience. I found a very traumatic imprint early in her life, something that had to be unspoken, unacknowledged. We reimprinted it and it was a very powerful change for her.

She came up to the present, and she felt an immense relief to be free from the imprint. But a few weeks later she began having an interesting experience. She said that she began to get a sense of very profound irrelevance because all of these behaviors, all of these aspects of her identity that had been built around this early imprint no longer had any meaning. She had built these protective mechanisms for herself so fully that she was willing to go to mental hospitals to hold on to them. Now, when she looked back at it all, she realized that she didn't need them anymore.

She didn't know what to do with all this behavior and this part of her identity. She had developed a whole way of being that now seemed completely unnecessary. She didn't want to go back to her old way of being to feel a sense of purpose, but still had to deal with a whole part of her that no longer had any purpose. She could even see now why people thought that was acting crazy.

What was she to do? She had this part that she just couldn't throw away. All these capabilities, those ways of acting, were still a part of her identity. The question was, *how was she to integrate them into her behavior in a way that had relevance to the present and future?*

I had her begin to work on **finding the positive value of this part of her** so that she could begin to integrate it into her future.

I will go over some of the ways we did that in the next demonstration.

My point is that **making a big change,** solving a problem that has been there for a long time, also **puts a person into another crisis,** another transition. **And her new SELF and her old SELF were not coordinated, were not integrated yet.**

When I was first working with my mother on the issue of her breast cancer, the very first thing that I noticed happening to her was that she was very incongruent about her identity. This is very interesting if you think of the metaphor of cancer.

Cancer is a part of you, a part of your identity, a part of your body that is running wild, out of control. It is a part of you, but it is not a part of you.

Often, many of the major illnesses that we have—at least the ones that today are not medically curable—have to do with this issue of body identity, which also relates to personal identity, and in particular to the immune system. The immune system is the part of the body responsible for its identity. The immune system distinguishes self from not-self, then removes what is not-self. Things like arthritis, allergies, cancer, AIDS, even some types of heart disease and diabetes, are all diseases that are a function of the immune system making a mistake.

Sometimes it doesn't recognize an invader as an invader; other times your body itself is perceived as an invader—as in arthritis, lupus, or multiple sclerosis. The immune system is attacking the body's joints in arthritis. It attacks its own nervous system in multiple sclerosis. In AIDS the immune system is attacking itself.

In some ways my experience working with people with that kind of health problem has been that there is often a similar kind of conflict happening in their own individual psychological identities as well. Certainly, when somebody is in a conflict with himself, he can't fully organize all his resources towards the goal of health.

In my mother's case it was an interesting conflict. She developed her cancer when her youngest son (the last of five children) was leaving home. She had been a mother for over thirty years, and all of a sudden she was in a transition to when this identity was no longer going to exist.

She had a part of her, an identity that was built around the role of mother. And for all these years she had sorted by others. She had put herself aside, had taken care of other people very competently, but there was a part of her, an individual side that sorted by self, that hadn't been allowed to grow for years.

As her children began to leave and she earned time for herself, what she actually did to fill that extra time was to start taking jobs in nursing. She was taking care of others again. There was a conflict between the part of her that knew what to do to be a mother, and that part of her that wanted to do things for herself. She wanted to travel, and go places, and do things.

The problem was that this mother identity, this other-oriented belief system said that the self-oriented part of her was selfish, and was not what her mission was. Her mission was to take care of other people.

The self-oriented side believed that the other-oriented side was being a martyr. It was always letting other people control her life, and never letting her do what she wanted to do.

An interesting thing will happen when somebody is in conflict with his identity like that. Any little thing can set off the conflict.

When somebody is completely congruent, all kinds of things can be going wrong in the world, and he can handle it very well. But if somebody is incongruent and in conflict in himself, any little thing can trigger stress.

In other words, if he breaks his fingernail, he will shout at himself, "What a stupid person, what a silly thing to do! Now my whole day is ruined."

It is not what happens on the outside that creates stress. Stress, especially the kind that causes illness, comes from the way we *respond* to what happens on the outside.

In my mother's case, if she had said, "Oh, maybe I should go out to dinner tonight, that would be something nice," the other side might say, "No, you should save the money, your children might need it sometime." Or some other reason: "It is selfish to do that."

So she would decide to stay home for dinner. And then her other part would go, "See, you never do anything, you are not happy, you can't go anywhere, you only think about others."

Anything that you try to make a decision about is a function of your identity. And **when there are conflicts about who you really are, neither choice is right.** If you choose this side, then you get the stress from that side. If you choose that side you get the stress and the bad feelings from this side. And you feel that you can't ever make the right decision.

When my mother looked into the future and imagined herself lying in a coffin, it actually looked rather peaceful. When you talk about building a will to live, you have to have an image of the future that fits with your mission. If the person sees being dead just as well as being alive, then in what kind of soil are you planting the seed?

This conflict was really no longer about the past. It was about, *WHO AM I? What is my mission? How do I get these to be parts of myself, these two identities to work together?*

Each one of them was trying to get rid of the other, to kill the other in that respect. So what we want to work with is how to get parts, such as conflicting beliefs, to live in harmony.

As I said before, it is no coincidence that we call a recovery from a life-threatening illness a "re-mission."

Beliefs in Conflict

What we want to work with is how to get two such conflicting identities or conflicting belief systems into harmony. We get conflicts in a system of beliefs when two or more beliefs lead to conflicting behaviors. This kind of situation often creates a "double bind" (where you are damned if you do and damned if you don't).

The most serious conflicts happen when conflicting beliefs involve identity problems with a negative judgement on oneself. This kind of conflict will almost always be the origin of problems involving *mistrust, hatred, or fear of oneself.* In most of those belief conflicts, we note oppositions between *logic and emotion, rationality and intuition, child and adult, past and future, change and stability.* It is the famous duality of YIN and YANG in Taoism.

Identifying the Conflict

I would also like to show some other ways in which we can elicit beliefs. *We will go back to our time line;* very often conflicts will come between the development of a new identity, a new you or secret you, and either the *present you* or other parts of you. We will mainly use three positions on the time line.

R.: Chris, you had asked about conflicts in yourself. Would you like to come up here?

(Chris comes and sits down on a chair.)

R.: Chris, the first thing I want to find out about you is *what the outcome is; the goal you have?*

C.: *I want to help people succeed.*

R.: So you want to help others succeed. We notice here that this is a sort by others. I want you to first build the soil for this new identity, this new belief.

This means that we want *to build a really good representation of what this outcome is.* If somebody is ill, for example, and he wants to be healthy, we want to build a full, rich representation of health.

Step 1: Representation of the outcome

R.: Chris, this is the time line in front of you. To your right is the future, to your left is the past. I first want you to stand up onto the line and, instead of going to the past as we did in the previous section, *go into the future and build a representation, a time and a situation where you would have been able to fully reach your goal.*

For example, if somebody wants to lose weight, he would walk on the line going to the future point where he would say, *"this is where I would be the weight and body shape I want to be."* So he is going to look into the future, and build a resource until he fully has what this outcome is all about associated in the experience.

R.: (To Chris): Go ahead, go at your own rate of speed.

[Robert points out a direction towards Chris' future.]

This is the new YOU that you want to develop. I want you to walk into that new you that is able to have all of these resources.

(To the audience): We want, of course, to watch the physiology, the body posture, gestures, and asymmetries.

[Chris walks slowly along the line, straightens up, and stops. His physiology is changed.]

R: As you experience yourself here, I would like you to visualize what it would be like; listen to the voice that you would use, and where you would speak from, really feel your posture, your physiology, your movement, so you know fully what it would be like to be in that future.

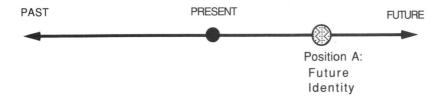

Figure 18. Creating an Associated Representation of the Goal State

[Robert puts his left hand on Chris' right shoulder as an anchor for this physiology.]

Step 2: Representation of the outcome from meta-position

Step back off the time line and go back *to the present now. And from the present, I would like you to look at this person, this future YOU.*

[Robert brings Chris back into the present and gets him out of the time line so he can be in the B dissociated position, sitting on his chair.]

R: Can you see and hear this YOU?

(To the audience): We start by saying, *this is the belief, the identity the person wants to have.* "I want to be able to help people succeed."

(To Chris): The next question is really simple: *What stops you? This is your future, this is your next step towards your mission.*

(To the audience): Think about it this way: People will say, "Oh, this outcome is wonderful, this is great!"

Then you come back to the present and say, "There it is, it is so wonderful, get it, go for it." Then you get, "Well, hum..."

That is the part that we want to find now—what is the conflict here?

(To Chris): When you look at that future, do you have a voice, a feeling? Something inside you shows its disagreement, its opposition.

C.   *Everything...* (mumbles)

(Robert says aloud for Chris, who muttered a few words to him): He says that it is something like, *if you succeed you distort your mission.*

Step 3: Finding the conflicting belief System

(To Chris): I want to find the part that has this belief. And *I would like you to put this part onto your time line where it most fits.*

Is it way back in the past? Is it near the present? Where on this line does this belief come from? Stand up and locate the place physically.

[Chris steps on his time line and, facing his future, goes back in his past and stops where his limiting belief was created. Chris walks slowly along his time line in a very deep silence. His hands are joined in front of his breast as if he was praying.]

(Robert, to the audience, in a very low voice at the beginning): By the way, while he is doing that, notice where the levels of the conflicts are. It is very common that in the future somebody wants a capability such as: *I want to be able to help others do this.*

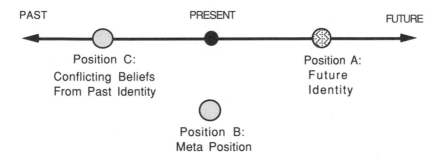

Figure 19. Location of Conflicting Beliefs.

But what it is conflicting with is a belief about the mission. Obviously, the motivation to develop this capability, if it conflicts with my mission, is going to be overridden.

If I can fit this capability in with my mission, then it becomes a part of my identity and it becomes natural and easy.

The same thing will happen with people trying to get well from an illness.

I want to be well, but it doesn't fit with my identity. I want to be well, but I can't because that is a selfish desire.

Here we have an interesting belief: *If I succeed on this capability level, I will fail with my mission.* That is a classic conflict.

(To Chris): Did you find anything, Chris?

C.:   *A moment.*

R.:   Alright, a moment, so not something really specific?

[Robert puts his right hand on Chris' left shoulder as an anchor for this feeling from the past, and shows him the direction of the future.]

So from this place you say, *that future goal conflicts with my mission, that will distort it.*

C.:   *A voice tells me, "You'd better look after you, not after the others."*

R.:   This part is saying, *You should be looking after you and not after the others. Be more self-oriented, not other-oriented.*

(To the audience): Notice the difference in physiology in this position. It is quite different from the physiology associated with the future.

Step 4: Identifying criteria from Meta Position

(To Chris): Step out of this spot and go back to the present meta-position.

[Chris comes back on his line to his present and gets out of it to be dissociated in position B. He sits down on his chair.]

(To Chris): Now visualize this part of yourself in your past, so you can see this one who says, "It's not good to want to help others to succeed."

And from where you are, I would like you to be able to see not only that "you from the past" on your time line, but also that "you in your future" on that other spot on your time line. From where you are, in that chair, you are neither of them for the time being.

Here is the one from the future who says, "I really want to help others succeed," and there is the one from the past who says, "No, it is dangerous, think of yourself first."

What are the criteria that one has in your past? What are its values?

And it is alright if you can't put words on it just now, but I want to be sure that you will stay out of either of them for the moment.

Step 5: Finding positive intentions

What we have is *two conflicting identities, separated,* and placed where they belong. Now we want to resolve the conflicts in the belief system.

[From each position A, B, C, Chris will tell about beliefs and values of each identity in A and C and what each of them thinks about the other. The B position, dissociated, will mainly help explain behaviors of A and C. Robert will lead the process towards the expression of positive intentions. He will go up the level of values until there is no more conflict between the parts.]

From position A

R.: (To Chris): I would like you to come here to your future, to be yourself in your future and to think about that one back there in your past that blocks your future.

[Chris moves to future position A.]

(To audience): Notice again the difference in the physiology.

(To Chris): What do you think of that part of you back there? Do you like it? Is it silly? What is it? Is it danger-ous? What do you think about it?

C.: *It makes a mistake. It is wrong.*

R.: Why does it make a mistake? *Why do you believe that about it?*

C.: *I think that it is afraid, that's all.*

R.: So when you look at that one, this part of you says, "That one is afraid." I get the impression from this side that this one sort of says, "Well, in fact it is insignificant, almost. It is not important." Is it important?

C.: *No.*

R.: (To audience): I would like to try something else for a moment. When Chris stands in his future facing the future, he sees this part of himself behind him as mistaken and insignificant. But what if he were to stand in his future facing the past?

(To Chris): I want you to look at this part of your past from this perspective. From this place in your future where you are, turn and face your past. What does this part of you in the future believe about that one over there in your past now?

(To audience): The change of physiology is interesting, isn't it?

C.: *I think I am able to help that one.*

R.: So from here in your future looking back, this part says, "I am able to help that one from the past."

From position C

Let's step off your time line for a moment. Now let's go back to this one here in your past and look at the future you.

[Chris comes back on the time line to his chair, then to the position C, in his past.]

R.: *What do you think about that one in the future?* Do you like it? Are you afraid of it? Why are you afraid of it? You don't know? What do you think about it? What are you afraid of? *What would happen if you were not afraid?*

C.: *I would cooperate.*

R.: What would happen then? What would happen if you cooperated?

C.: *I don't know.* (Chris' eyes are looking down.)

R.: (To audience): Once again, you can see the difference between two physiologies, especially at the accessing cue level between the representations of the two identities: the past one is kinesthetic, the future one is visual.

By the way, it is one thing to be afraid of a spider or a snake. When you are around the spider, then you are uncomfortable. But if you are afraid of yourself you can't ever escape, no matter how thick the walls you build or how high a mountain you climb, you can't get away from what you are afraid of.

Think deeply, Chris. *What is the belief? What would you lose?*

Long silence, then:

C.: *I have a deep sense of sadness.*

R.: Come back to meta-position and leave all that behind.

From position B

[Chris comes back dissociated in B position and sits down on his chair.]

R.: Now this one in the future looks back and says, "I can help that one, it just made a mistake."

This one from the past is afraid of that future one. It is not really sure why. When we say, "What would happen if you cooperated?", what comes up is a deep sense of sadness. Why would sadness happen when you think of cooperating? *What is sadness usually about? Loss?*

This one says, "If I do that I will lose something in some way."

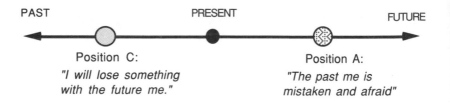

Figure 20. Identification of the Limiting Beliefs

I don't know if this is the case for Chris, but sometimes it is. "I give up myself, I sell out myself. Maybe this was a mistake back here but it is me."

One interesting paradox that often happens is that as we get older and more resourceful we develop all kinds of new capabilities and behaviors, but often our identity was decided somewhere back early in childhood. So even though you have these capabilities, when you use them it feels as if you are being a fake.

"I am doing those things now but my past is the real ME."

"This sad scared little boy is the real me."

"All of this present ability is a fake. I can go through the motions, but it is not really me, and if I changed into an adult I would be giving up me."

Some people feel that if they really changed, a part of them would die. And, in a sense, *maybe that old identity would die.* The feeling can be quite strong.

I remember working with another person who had been labeled schizophrenic. She tended to swing between being depressed and morose to having violent outbursts. When we got down to the core of the system that was creating her problems, she had a belief that went something like: *If I want to be like other people, then I lose myself. I disappear.*

Given her family system, that was a necessary belief in order for her to develop any kind of identity. But notice the underlying structure of the belief. *"I am not* other people. I have to be the polarity of whatever is happening around me. If people are happy I am sad and catatonic. If people are quiet and still I am boisterous and making noise. I have to do whatever is the opposite of what everyone else is doing or I don't exist."

That drove this woman's life. So she was always acting inappropriately in any situation. This woman felt that if she didn't do that, she didn't exist, she would die. And her terror of that feeling, of not existing, was certainly stronger than whatever punishment she got for acting inappropriately.

Notice that she said, "If I even *want to be like* somebody else," which meant that if she started to like somebody and wanted to be like them, then she also didn't exist. If you started liking people, then they would suck out your identity—even if you just *wanted* to be like them, whether you actually acted like them or not.

By the way, you realize that typical N.L.P. rapport techniques won't work anymore then, because as soon as you get rapport with them, they don't exist anymore. And *that is the kind of belief that will create what people call **psychosis** or mental illness.

(To Chris, still sitting on his chair): I bring that up in this context, Chris, because I think that in order to understand some of this fear and sadness that is directed at yourself, it is important to recognize those kinds of identity decisions and identity beliefs.

From out here and staying dissociated, I would like you to look at this old part of you that is sad and frightened, as well as that part in the future that is full of resources and ready to help, without you being any of them. See them from far away, see them from high up.

When you look at this one from your past, do you understand anything about it? *What do you understand about its intention?*

C.:   *I would say something like survival; "You must survive."*

R.: (To audience): This one is afraid for survival. That one in his future wants to go ahead and help people. Very often you will find parts of people that object to their own behavior: "I don't like what *that one* does; that one scares me," or "What it is capable of scares me."

The first thing you want to do in any negotiation, whether it is between two people in a company or parts of yourself, is **to find the values that they are operating from.** Purposes and intentions are what direct activities.

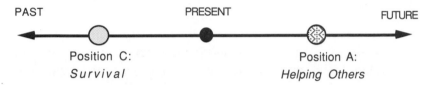

Figure 21. Identification of the Criteria of the Conflicting Parts

You will often find that people won't disagree with the other person's intentions or values once they know what they are. In fact, you might actually find that they share values. You must forget about judging this one's behavior, or what it knows, or doesn't know, and go to the level of criteria and values.

Step 6: Finding the common objective

From position A

R.: (To Chris): Come up to here, in your future, in A; I would like you to look at that one over there in your past.

That one back there is sad and afraid of you, and it has an intention of survival. Do you not want it to survive?

C.: *Yes, I do.*

R.: You do want it to survive. So your purpose isn't to threaten its survival. What is your purpose? *What is your intention? What is the value that you chose? What is your mission?*

C.: *To succeed.*

R.: (To audience): The criterion is to succeed. What is the purpose of succeeding? I am asking this question because I want to go to an even deeper criterion.

Notice that here in A we have action, capability, and activity; and there in B we have survival, identity.

Whether you are in business, or working with people, or a family, you often find this conflict between the part that wants to be creative, do new things, and take risks, and this part that is afraid of losing stability and identity.

(To Chris): "What is the intention of success?"

C.: *To feel useful.*

R.: And I guess it would be difficult to feel useful if you didn't survive.

C.: *Yes.*

R.: Now go back into that part of you from your past. [Chris walks to position C.]

From position C

R.: Do you hear what that future one says? It says, "I don't want to challenge your survival. My goal is to feel useful, to be successful, but also to survive."

Do you believe that one? Or do you not trust it?

C.: *I can't see how it can do that.*

R.: (To audience): This one literally says, "I don't *see* how." It doesn't surprise me, by the way, from Chris' eye position. This past part is very kinesthetic.

(To Chris): Your purpose is survival. That doesn't necessarily conflict with success, does it? Or usefulness? What good is survival if one can't be useful and growing, and successful, and happy at the same time? Besides, in order to really survive I often need to do new things.

In other words, what helps me to survive as a child is different from what helps me to survive as an adult.

And if the criterion really is survival, survival involves adaptation to new situations and building new resources. You can't survive if you don't develop something new.

You can think about that for a moment, then come out to meta-position. [Chris comes back to his chair, sits down, and remains lost in his thoughts.]

Step 7: The resources to share

R.: (To audience): We have taken this future goal and raised the level of values that support that goal. This is not just a goal now, it is actually related to deeper values.

The crux of the problem now is: *This future one is sitting up here with all this capability but no depth of identity. This past one has these very profound feelings but no capability.*

That is a common thing that happens in our lives. A younger person is capable of very deep feelings and deep decisions, but doesn't always have the capabilities. That's why it says, "I need to see how."

R.: (To Chris): So here is what we are going to do: I would like you to look at each of these two parts from your dissociated position here in the present and see what resources each one has, from out here.

What resources does this one in your future have that the other one doesn't have?

C.: *The knowledge, the way to, the know-how.*

R.: Now, there is the other important question: What does that one in your past have that this one doesn't have and needs?

C.: (Mumbles.)

R.: He says, "Guts?"

That is important. This one has been looked at as always afraid. But this one has guts. I mean that this one is willing to stand behind what it believes, right or wrong, regardless of what anyone else says.

Think about the kind of effort and commitment it takes to lose weight, quit smoking, or start a new business. It takes more than vision and know-how; it takes energy and guts.

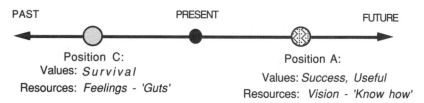

Figure 22. Core Values and Resources of Conflicting Parts

Step 8: Integration of the new identity

Here is what I would like to do. You can see from here that these both really need each other. You can see that their purposes don't conflict. They both want survival and a better life.

Transfer of resources from C to A

Go into this one from the past; I want you to reach deeply into that sense of feeling, that depth, those guts, and that energy.

[Robert touches anchor associated with past identity.]

I would like you to walk slowly towards this future you, taking that sense of feeling with you. So that in the end you bring that feeling into the physiology of the future you. You are going to bring this resource from the past... all the way to this one. Make sure that you go all the way into this one.

[Chris' physiology changes as he moves up his time line, ending with his future state physiology—although the future state physiology has changed to incorporate some physiology from the younger Chris.]

Transfer from A to C

Now I would like you to take this future one's vision and know-how and take it back into that earlier you, holding that know-how and that capability to help others succeed, but bringing it back to help your other younger self succeed.

[Robert touches anchor associated with future state.]

Bring these abilities to the you from your past and completely go into this "you of the past."

[Chris walks from future position to past position with much emotion. His physiology becomes like his younger self, but with parts of his future state physiology.]

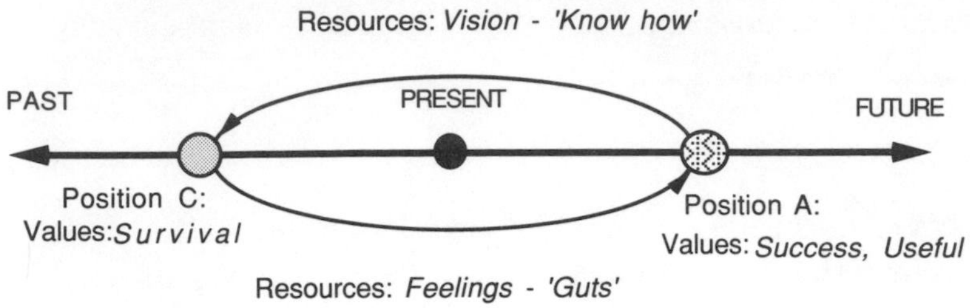

Resources: *Vision - 'Know how'*

PAST   PRESENT   FUTURE

Position C: Position A:
Values:*Survival*   Values: *Success, Useful*

Resources: *Feelings - 'Guts'*

Figure 23. Transfer of Resources Between the Conflicting Parts

Back here, in your past, you can now "see how" those resources have melted together.

So the two ways of thinking will be fully integrated.

(To audience): He is already starting to change his physiology quite dramatically, as you can see.

Back in B

Step 9: Integration of past and future belief systems

Now let's go back to meta-position and test to make sure there is no more disagreement. As if leading each part by hand, we can help them come even closer, to merge into a new identity on the time line in your present.

As you look at them both from meta-position, I would like to have you see the one that has been so far away from the other, and watch them coming closer together.

In fact, I would like you to imagine you are taking them both in your hands in order *to bring them together now.*

Step 10: Total integration

In just a moment, when you are ready, I want you to take the full image, the full picture that you have here in your

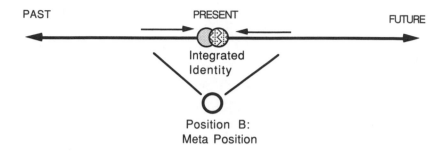

Figure 24. Integration of Conflicting Parts

present portraying the integration of both parts of your identity. I would like you to take this position and with that depth, guts, energy, vision, and knowledge, step into this integrated you in the present. Then walk towards the future. You have the past, you have the present, and the future.

[With his eyes closed, Chris walks towards his future state, stumbles slightly but then regains his balance, and then walks confidently to the future state.]

That's OK; sometimes you trip over something along the way but... *the future is yours!*

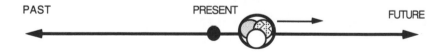

Figure 25. Future Pacing New Identity 'Molecule'

Comments

I think that the same kind of dynamic conflict can occur in a family, or in management situations. The more the father says to the son, "Come on, you are capable, don't be stupid and afraid, don't be a weakling, you made a mistake, you are wrong to be afraid," the more the son has to prove *he is not wrong by being afraid, etc.*

In other words, the less the son is understood, the more he has to hold on to his belief to maintain his identity. Of course, the more the son holds on, the harder the father pulls and pulls. The father creates a context in which, in order for the son to succeed in the task, he has to lose in the relationship. So each forces the other to a further separation without realizing it.

But if they can then jump to a level of sharing values, they might be able to find what their beliefs about each other in the relationship are. They have a new awareness from which to find a resolution.

In Chris' case one part of him thought that the other made a mistake, and was just kind of weak and afraid. But the thing that part was able to realize was that his younger self didn't make a mistake at the level of identity. And in fact the strength that it used to hold on to that identity for so many years is exactly the kind of strength that his future self needs in order to be able to do what it wants to do. It is sitting up here and thinking that it has everything figured out, but doesn't realize the guts that are needed to do that.

From meta-position, we have this new perspective from which both parts can see that they do share the same values. They are not different MEs, they are not different identities. From out here, they can see that they are really joined, they are really the same on this level of identity. They are me; all of it is me.

From meta-position we can see that this younger one has resources that the other one in fact could use and learn from; and the older one has resources that this younger one could use and learn from. The solution is not the older one saying, "Don't be stupid, you are making a mistake, don't hold me back." But, "You have something that I need, I would never want to leave you behind."

Sometimes the members of a system that desire success think, "Ah, if I have any feeling of sadness, or any feeling of fear, then I fail." They don't realize that those feelings are what add depth to your success. Many people say, "Success, success, success..." ignoring the other most important side of life, the depth of life. Feeling sad, even feeling weak adds depth. The depth of fear gives a depth to the success. If I know exactly what I am facing, I can feel the sense of fear, the sense of sadness, and go forward anyway.

I see some people do N.L.P. who try to ignore sadness or fears as if to say, "Just turn away, focus on your outcome and forget about your fear, go for it!"

But true depth is having all of that. It is embracing what all life is about. And if you can't feel weakness in yourself, if you can't relate to their sense of fear, to their sense of sadness, how can you help other people succeed?

As Don Juan said to Carlos Castaneda, "Being a warrior is being able to fully address both the terror and the wonder of being a human being."

If you only address one side, there is no depth.

Steps of the Process

I would like to review the steps of the process.

1. I step on to my time line. Take the belief or the identity that I want to develop for the future, and deepen the soil for this identity to grow in by making an associated representation of what it will be like. It's like a very powerful form of future pacing.

2. Then I step out of the future state and find the limiting belief or identity by asking, "What stops me? This is wonderful, this is a great outcome, so what stops me?"

   Maybe it is a feeling, words, or some other form of impasse.

3. I find the place on the time line where this limiting belief belongs. I establish that position by associating into it.

4. Then I come out to a third position where I am in neither of them, where I can see them both.

   From that position, I have calibrated to the physiology of both the identities. I want to create this perspective from a third position where I can see them both.

5. Then I go inside each position, looking at the other to find and bring out the beliefs. What does this side think of that one? What does this side believe about that one? Then I come back out to the third position. Now I realize that these beliefs may not be accurate.

6. I want to find the intention behind each part and keep finding deeper and deeper values until I find the place where they both join, where neither of them conflicts. This one says, "My intention is not to threaten you, it is to change, to grow, to succeed."

   The other answers, "My intention is not to hold you back, it is to survive."

   At the intention level, there is really no conflict.

7. From the third position I explore the values, the criteria, the intentions. And from the third position I ask, "What are the resources that each of them has, that are needed by the other?" So that after I have explored them both and gone into them a few times, I can perceive each of them as valuable.

Sometimes people think one side is a bad part of themselves. "It is always punishing me, or holding me back."

But you begin to realize that this seemingly negative side will often have a good intention. Its behavior may not be the best way to satisfy the intention, but this intention is needed.

The negative side can also have a lot of power. There is a funny paradox I sometimes encounter in which people will say, "This part is weak."

But there is often a lot of strength in that weakness because it can stop them from doing anything. That weakness is power. And if that power was aligned with you instead of against you, then nothing could stop you.

8. I want to take the resource from each part to the other. I usually start from the objecting side. I take the vision and the belief that they really are working together, that they share an identity and an intention, from the third position into the objecting part of the identity. Then I take that part's resources and physically move them and bring them into the physiology of the other position. That is a very interesting experience. Then I take the other one's resources, its capabilities, and I do the same thing; I bring them back to the other part.

9. Now that each shares what the other has, I finally go to the third position and bring them together to make one new image, one new identity. Then I put that on my time line in

the present, not only to see it from the outside, but associating into it. Then I go back into the future.

Anchors

You can use anchors to help the integration process. Anchor future state A, and anchor past state C. In Chris' case I put them on different shoulders, then I held the appropriate anchor to help bring resources from one position to the other.

Comments

Bringing resources back and forth is often a very interesting experience.

Usually I find the biggest fear that these two have about each other is that one says, "The problem with that one is that it is not me, it doesn't have what I have."

And this one says, "The reason I am afraid of that one is that it doesn't think like me."

In other words, this one says, "I am afraid to cooperate with the other because I don't see any of myself in it. I will lose myself and my needs because the other one doesn't share them. So I have to fight for my side of the relationship." Part of Chris was saying, "If I acknowledge that one I might get lost in all this depth of sadness and fear." But if this one had the resources and capabilities of the other there wouldn't be a problem!

It is like parents who are afraid of their child going out on his own until they see some of themselves in the child. But then, instead of actually teaching and giving their capabilities to the child, they criticize and punish the child for not having them, which of course makes the split grow further.

So I think balancing their resources begins to create a trust between them.

"I can trust you because I know that you think like me now."

"I can trust you because I know that you share my values."

In a sense that is what trust is. "Knowing that you consider me and think like me, so I can trust that you won't forget it." I can love my neighbor as myself only after I share myself with my neighbor, and have put myself in my neighbor's shoes.

SUMMARY OF BELIEF SYSTEMS INTEGRATION EXERCISE

Conflicts in belief systems occur when two or more presently existing beliefs lead to behaviors that are contradictory. This type of situation often creates a "double bind" (where you are "damned if you do and damned if you don't"). The most problematic conflicts occur when the opposing beliefs involve identity issues around which there is a negative judgment about oneself. This kind of conflict will almost always be at the root of a problem that involves a mistrust/hatred/fear/etc. of oneself.

1. Identify the conflicting beliefs or identity issues your partner has. Have your partner step into the location on his or her time line that most represents where that belief or identity was formed. Common types of conflicts include logic vs. emotion, rational vs. intuitive, childhood beliefs vs. adult beliefs, past vs. future, etc.

   Calibrate the physiology of each of the identities in conflict. Pay particular attention to asymmetries of movements and gestures.

2. Have the subject establish a "meta-position" at a location that is off the time line and dissociated from either of the beliefs or identities.

3. Have your partner step into each location and ask each part to look at the other and describe what it thinks of the other.

At this stage the different parts (identities) will typically dislike and distrust the others.

4. Find the *positive intention* and *purpose* of each part. Make sure that each part recognizes and accepts the positive intent of the other.

   From "meta-position" find the common mission that both parts actually share.

5. Have each part look at the other again and this time describe the *resources* that the other has that would be helpful to that part to accomplish its own positive intention and the common mission.

   a. Secure a congruent agreement from the parts to *combine their resources* so they can more fully accomplish their own purposes and the common mission. Usually the reason that they will have mistrusted or disliked each other previously is precisely because the other has not had these resources and has thus seemed foreign and out of control.

   b. Keep an eye out for other limiting beliefs at this stage that have not surfaced previously and that will need to be refined or updated. For example, "It isn't possible to be responsible *and* enjoy myself at the same time."

6. Ask your partner to step into each part (starting with the one in the earliest time location); focus on the special resources of the part and slowly walk on the time line, carrying those resources, and step into the location of the other part—so that each part has within it the resources of the other. (Calibrate to an integration/symmetry of the two psychologies that accompanied the separate identities.)

7. Have your partner step to "meta-position" and visualize the two parts joining together to become a single identity in the

present. Step into that integrated identity and walk towards the future.

[NOTE: Sometimes a conflict may involve more than two identity issues. In such a case you may either expand this technique to include all three or do the integrations two at a time.]

Comments After the Exercise

One comment is based on what I noticed in one group. I think it is important to realize that *sometimes a major conflict is not necessary between the future and the past.*

Sometimes, for instance, a person is being stopped from going into the future by guilt from the past. If you think about what guilt is for a moment, you realize that *guilt is a blaming of yourself.* It *needs* a part that is doing the blaming and a part that is being blamed. So that *the thing keeping you from going to the future isn't necessarily an objection from the past to the future. It may be some imprint from the past where you split off two parts of yourself, and they are in conflict back there.*

You are first saying, "I am trying to go to this future goal, but this thing from the past stops me." Sometimes when you get back there, you find that there is actually a past conflict that is holding you back. So you do the integration between these two parts from the past.

There are certain types of beliefs or issues that can give you a clue to that: *Guilt* is one, *lack of trust in self* might be another.

But the thing I want to bring out is: Do the integration where the conflict actually is.

Link between Values and Beliefs

Q.: *What is the link between values and beliefs?*

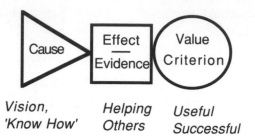

Figure 26. Structure of a Belief

Values fit into beliefs. But the value itself is not the whole belief. Beliefs tend to have a structure that goes like this:

So some cause makes an effect, then *this effect becomes evidence of some value or criterion.* The value may be success, or it could be survival.

"Doing this will cause me to be effective with other people."

Then I have my *criterial equivalence,* the *evidence.* "How do I know that I am successful or useful? How do I know that I am surviving, that I am going to survive or be effective?"

Of course, what will often happen is that I get *two criteria or values that are based on the same evidence.*

For example, this means that *I am successful,* but it also means that *my survival is threatened.* So the evidence becomes confusing because it points to both. That is why we want to use these techniques to sort that kind of confusion out.

Values are more abstract than the evidence for the accomplishment of the value. "If I have a certain amount of money, I am a successful person," or "If my employees like me, then I am a successful leader."

Criterial equivalences tend to be more sensory-based than a criterion or value. The belief is actually the definition of these relationships.

> *The belief is neither the cause, nor the evidence, nor the value. It is the definition of their relationships.*

So when I am working with a belief, the belief might change either because I suddenly point out that this cause will produce a negative outcome, or because new evidence comes up and changes the meaning of the value. Let's say someone has the belief that "punishment causes motivation," or that somebody has to be punished in order to change. He could come to realize that punishment is causing other things that actually work against a person's incentive; or he may redefine the evidence for motivation or change to be based on internal feelings as well as external responses, and the whole relationship is rearranged.

Q.: *What if the future situation seems impossible to the person?*

When one part says, "Everything is possible," usually you will find right away that there is another part that says, "Nothing is possible." The more that this one goes, "Nothing is possible," the more the other one separates itself and goes, "Everything is possible."

Again, the goal of the belief integration process is the same for both. I want to find out what their two intentions are. If I can bring this dreamer's vision to this critic, and this critics sensibility to this dreamer, then I can create something that is realistic. I say, "Fine, that dream is necessary. As long as it is integrated, so that I can do it in a real and whole way." A house divided against itself won't stand.

If I get caught up trying to figure out whether it is possible or not myself, I am just promoting the conflict. People thought it was impossible to get to the moon fifty or sixty years ago. It takes a lot of realism and commitment to fulfill a dream that is that big.

Q.: *In some work on polarity we were doing in gestalt, we went through the emotion of opposition between the two parts. To do this technique, do we have to avoid these emotions in going into a meta-position?*

Obviously not. We certainly didn't avoid those kinds of emotions in Chris' case. The idea is that conflict doesn't create the meta-position; understanding the positive intention of the parts involved in the conflict is what creates the true meta-position.

The emotions are driven by the intention, the identity, and the values of the person. The difference between what we are doing and what Fritz Perls did is in *specifically working with the meta-position. We are making a meta-position.* We don't want just the two chairs, because we have to get outside of that whole thing. And instead of just trying to sort it out by the emotions, we want to jump all of the levels and use all of the senses.

The solution comes from creating a context outside of the conflict.

The emotion is important in order to convince me that the person is really associated into this position. If I tell the person, "Go into the stuck state," and the person goes, and says, "OK!" but there is no significant change in physiology; this is not going to get me anything. *I want to see them BE IT,* which means there has to be physiology, emotions, everything else.

Emotions are a function of relationships. Emotions tell you about a relationship. The same two parts that create guilt when they oppose each other, create peace when they support each other. It is not like guilt and peace are different things. Emotion is an energy that is directed by relationships between parts of ourselves.

If I take anger, which has been turned on myself, and turn it towards a vision, it becomes commitment. Anger isn't a thing that you can put in a box and go, "Oh, this is anger... oh, this is emotion." It is the way that these internal feelings are channeled. When I rearrange how they are working together it makes something different.

Fear turns into power. It is the same energy; it is just how it is directed.

I want people to go back into those emotions alright, but I also want to know how I am going to bring them together, so instead of draining each other's energy, they are supporting each other's energy. Again, it is the relationship that determines the quality of the feeling.

Fritz Perls was brilliant, but he needed some other structures to really know how to finish business. Richard Bandler once said, "All business is finished. The question is whether it got finished the way you wanted it to or not."

You can finish it poorly, or finish it well. *What has to happen to finish it well? This is where I think you need to look at relationships and bring in resources.*

I don't know if Perls ever had people give the resource from one part to the other one. This is not necessarily explicit in his work. I think this is a very important part of the resolution, though, so they share each other's experiences. Your emotions are important, but so is everything else.

Q.: *I am under the impression that the part from the past is trying to protect the person.*

Very often identity decisions are made when you are a child. They need to be updated as you mature.

What often happens is that we go through *stages of transition* in our lives, and these transitions, even if they are positive, create this sort of identity crisis. Becoming a parent makes a transition that is a change of identity. So does getting a new job. A lot of times in these transitions the identity has to be reevaluated or reintegrated.

I find that very often, especially if there is a quick transition, there is not really enough time for the old identity and the new identity to come together.

In many traditional cultures, this is the purpose of what they call "rites of passage." These rites are built into the culture for the purpose of integrating the identity between one phase and another.

Modern cultures have forgotten a lot about that important phase. Sometimes, we even make a new identity based on trying to get rid of an old identity.

"I don't want to be this anymore, so I will be everything that is the opposite of that old me." So for a while the development of the new identity is actually based on *going away from or being the opposite of the old identity.*

This strategy can be useful, but the old identity has to be reintegrated at some point. *You will probably mostly find that the earlier parts are more identity-related. And the later parts might be some new beliefs, or some new capabilities that have been developed as you evolve.* Therefore the earlier identity often seems to be in a protective position.

Q.: *You talked about how the belief changed, then the behavior changed later. The critical phase was when the belief and the behavior were the furthest apart from each other. I have often stated to others and myself that this specific moment was most suitable for illness. How can we help a person out in that phase?*

This is the value of what we have done in this exercise.

As I go into the future, I need to know that my behavior is not always going to immediately fit the new belief. That critical point is where I really need the strength and the support from the past. Because if I just try to make myself be this new person, and this past part of me doesn't believe "it is possible," then when I get to that place where the belief and the behavior are not together, I get pulled back by this one from the past. But if they are aligned, they provide that support and energy to make it to that critical mass that is needed for everything to come together.

So when I future pace, I want to make sure that the person knows that it is not necessarily just going to be all roses.

I think that just showing people this relationship between belief and performance sometimes really helps them to anticipate the natural cycle of change, so that they perceive the events around this critical point as feedback and not failure.

Another strategy is to go into the future beyond a particular outcome that the person has. So you are even further ahead, looking back onto what the potential problems were and how you dealt with them. If I look at it from this more distant future perspective, I might even see some ways to get past that critical point.

CHAPTER V

Belief Systems and Relationships

Probably the most effective way to get past the crisis point is by having a support system. We not only want to develop the behaviors and capabilities to support the belief, but to develop a support system in the environment.

One of the things that I would invite each of you to do is, as you **think of the new beliefs and new identity that you set for yourself, think for a moment of the place and people you can go to to develop support for that belief.**

Maybe there is a special place that you go to in order to be with yourself and reaffirm yourself. If you don't already have that kind of place, plan one; imagine where you will put it. Make one for yourself.

Also think of people who will most support your changes; make sure that you have trustable feedback and reinforcement for your changes. Change does not always have to be all on your shoulders. There are many people who will want to help you change and want to support you.

We must also consider that there are going to be people who are not going to support your change, perhaps because it threatens them. We need to have ways of dealing with that. I don't believe that unsupportive people are bad. I believe they have positive intentions; but the question is how to draw out that intention into supportive behavior.

I want to do a last demonstration around the issue of transforming non-supportive relationships.

I would like you to think of somebody that you anticipate having problems communicating with in relation to your desired belief change. Think of somebody you think you'll have a hard time getting along with. Does anybody have such a person?

Why don't you come up, Barbara?

(Barbara comes up.)

The Meta-Mirror

Step 1: Naming the Other's Behavior

R.: Imagine this person is right here in front of you.

Give a name to the behavior that really makes it difficult when you are around that person. What is it that he does? What would you call it? How does he act? Is he insensitive? Is he rigid?

B.: *Indifferent.*

Step 2: Naming Your Own Behavior

R.: Now, physically move to meta-position and observe your own response in relation to other person when he is indifferent. What would you call your own behavior?

B.: *Rigidity, maybe. Inflexibility would suit better.*

R.: So there is indifference in him and inflexibility in you. I would like you to consider this: could he still be indifferent if you were not inflexible? Would it be possible for

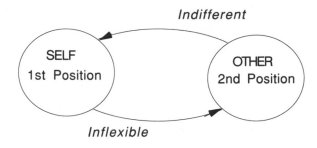

Figure 27. Diagram of Unsupportive Relationship

him to be indifferent if you were something other than inflexible? The point is this: in any human system what you do determines how other people act as much as what they do determines how you act.

Is this person indifferent to your behavior or to your identity?

B.: *To my identity.*

R: And what are you inflexible about?

B: *About what's important for me in the relationship.*

R: Your values?

B. *Yes.*

R.: (To audience) I want you to notice that the people that you probably have the most difficult times with are the ones that you allow to affect your identity.

I once modeled the strategy of a person whose job was basically to handle criticism from customers for his company. If people complained, he would always start at whatever level they were complaining at, and pace and lead them down to a specific behavior level.

Sometimes people criticize your identity, saying things like, "It was your fault." If you take it on an identity level and feel, "There is something wrong with me!", it is going to have a fairly big emotional effect on you. And you will burn out very quickly.

But this person would say something like, "I am sorry you are upset. Can you tell me what specifically happened?" It was redirecting the criticism from him to the problem. In fact, he stood towards the person who would be complaining like a martial artist. He used his physiology and his gestures to direct the words and pictures to a specific location away from his body. So they were focused on 'the problem' and not him.

Finally he moved it up on to their left to the memory location, and made it feedback as opposed to failure. He didn't take it at an identity level. He knew his identity was alright, regardless of what the response was. He didn't have to deny or fight the criticism; he directed it to where it would actually do the most good.

(Robert to Barbara): Maybe you are giving too much of yourself to this person?

B.:   *Yes.*

R.:   And your rigidity about your values hasn't made him any less indifferent to you?

B.:   *No, because I was sucked into his system. And now I'm, stuck. I can't get out.*

Step 3: The Relation between the Two Me's

Now I want you to physically move to a fourth position over here. When you look at how your inner meta-position self is trying to change your outer first position self, and the way you are communicating with that person, what is this relationship like? (Robert points successively at 1 and 3.)

B.: *Between* **me** *and* **me?**

R.: Yes. We want to explore the question, "How do I relate to myself in reference to the other person?"

B.: *The inner me thinks that nothing the outer me does is going to have any effect on that other person anyway.*

R.: In a way, you are doing to yourself what he is doing to you. The inner you also seems indifferent to the you stuck in that relationship. I call this process the meta mirror, because often the way the person is treating you is a reflection of how you treat yourself. The problem is not only the other person or even how I react to the other person, the problem is also here, in the system between the two me's. That is an important part of how the total system works.

How does the outer you react to that inner indifference?

B.: *She is very tense. She is afraid she will lose her identity.*

R.: No wonder the outer you is rigid. She's stuck between a rock and a hard place.

I think it might be interesting to switch these positions (the inner you and the outer you) around.

For example, what if you had switched the places of the first-position outer you with the inner meta position you,

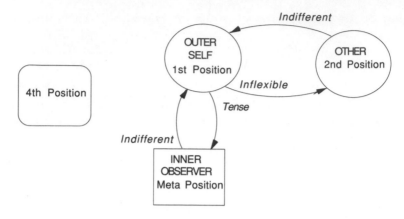

Figure 28. Diagram of Total Relational System

so that you were indifferent to the other person and inflexible about your values with yourself! Perhaps the more inflexible I am about my values with *me,* the more creative I can be in my behavior with him.

The nice thing about working systemically like this is that you don't have to change the elements of the system to find a solution. You only need to change the relationship between the elements. What if you did that? Just take these two and physically shift them around.

B.:   *It seems easy that way.* (Laughing)

R.:   What happens? Is the relationship the same?

B.:   *I think there is none now.*

R.:   And if there is no more relationship, then you can start a new one even if it's with the same person?

B.:   *Yes.*

R.:   Now let's come look at these two: this part that is in meta-position now, that is being inflexible about your values with yourself.

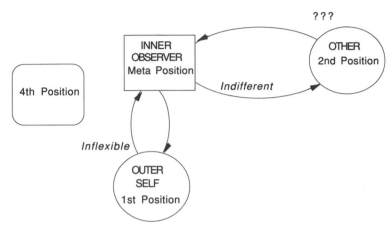

Figure 29. Shifting Perceptual Positions In the Unsupportive Relationship

Do you want to have a relationship with this person now?

B.: *No, not at all.*

R.: What kind of relationship would you make sure that you had here if you ever talked to that person in the future?

B.: *The trouble now is that I don't want to communicate anymore.*

R.: What would make you want to communicate?

B.: *A more sincere person, a bit more authentic.*

R.: OK. Now, put yourself into this other person's position for a moment; into second position. If you are experiencing the world as this person, what would make you a more sincere and authentic person?

[Barbara physically moves into the position of the other person. For a moment she is very deep in thought.]

B.: *Self-confidence.*

R.: Now come all the way out of this system to the fourth position. I want you to notice something important here.

If you bring confidence out of this other person, if you act in a way that makes him confident, then he is going to be more authentic. Here is the big question: How would you act to make him more confident that would still be in line with your own values?

B.:   *Certainly not by being inflexible.*

R.:   What way would it be?

B.:   *By being open and listening, at least.*

R.:   But also making sure that you keep your inflexibility about your values out here in the meta-position, because I want you to notice that "open and listening" is not indifferent to who I am and what is important to me. *Open and listening* is not going to be getting sucked in, especially if I am inflexible out here in third position.

So I can be more open and listening with that person because I have support from myself.

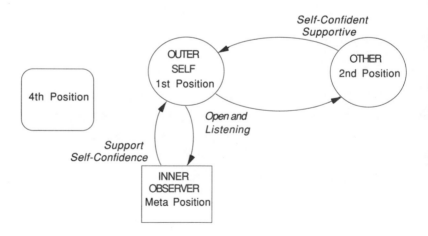

Figure 30. Diagram of the New Functional Support System

Step 4: Entering the New Relationship

R.:   From fourth position visualize the you in first position in this new relationship being open and listening to the other person—but supported by the meta-position you who knows who you are and is inflexible about your values and identity—step into the first position and look at that other person.

(Barbara steps to first position and laughs.)

R.:   (To the audience): Look at that physiology. It is an interesting combination of all of the other ones.

(To Barbara): What happens with that person?

B.:   *It is more comfortable.*

R.:   How do you feel?

B.:   *Much better. It is completely different.*

R.:   Thank you.

Very often the place that you have difficulty communicating with another person is a mirror image of how you are relating to yourself.

It is not really the other person who is either the problem or the solution.

If I can step back to see how it is really a reflection of my relation with myself, then I can restructure the system so that I am supporting myself. This will often transform the whole relationship. The meta mirror technique creates a context in which we can keep shifting perceptual positions inside and outside the problematic relationship until we find the most appropriate and ecological arrangement of elements in the relational molecule.

Summary of the Meta Mirror Technique

1. Identify a person you have difficulty communicating with. Visualize that person from first position (associated) and name the trait that makes communication so difficult. *e.g.,* *"rigid," "insensitive," "incongruent," "denial," etc.*

2. Step back to *meta position* (dissociated from the relationship) and visualize yourself in the interaction. Name your own behavior in relation to the other person. *e.g., "judgmental," "irritated," "helpful," "scared," etc.*

3. Notice how the way you are acting actually reinforces or triggers the behavior of the other person in the system. (If you were not there, how would the other person act? Could the other person continue his or her responses?)

4. Think of what other ways you could respond to that person. Perhaps you have tried to change your own reactions already. What makes you continue to act the way you do in this relationship?

5. Now take a step to the side (the *"meta-four" position*) and look at how you treat yourself in this interaction. *i.e., "pushy," "angry," "judgmental," "creative," etc.* Notice at which logical levels (behavior, capability, belief, identity) the different responses are operating.

   In what way is your response to yourself a mirror for what the other person is doing?

6. From the "meta-fourth" position, switch the two positions associated with yourself. That is, put your third-position reactions (the way you have been treating yourself) into the first position so you have that level of response to the other person. Put your former first-position responses into the third-position location.

Notice how the switch changes the system and transforms the expression of the responses.

7. Put yourself into the other person's shoes (second position). View yourself from the other person's eyes. How does your behavior appear from that perspective? From this other person's perspective, what do you need or want from yourself.

8. Reassociate into the revised first-position location (i.e., the one that has been replaced by the former third-position level reactions). Notice how your reactions and point of view have changed.

9. Continue to switch perspectives and add choices of responses (at the appropriate level) until you feel the relationship is more balanced and functional.

CHAPTER VI

Conclusion

Let's review all of the elements of working with beliefs that have been explored in this book.

We started by separating beliefs from the other functions in our lives and behavior. Beliefs are different from strategies and capabilities, different from behaviors, and we said that they had to do with generalizations about causes, meanings, values, and limits.

These are really a different level than behavior.

Arguing about behavior won't necessarily change the belief, because behavior is on another level.

We started by working with some simple beliefs about capability, finding that what gave them their power was not that they were a picture, a sound, or a feeling, but a molecule that was composed of relationships, a synesthesia among pictures, sounds, and feelings.

Our first step was to reorganize those representations into their appropriate physiological accessing positions.

Then we could restructure the relationship so that they supported each other in the system.

We then went a little deeper. As we got to more **major beliefs, core beliefs,** we found that they are not molecules made of just representational systems, but *of critical relationships between people.*

It might be the relational molecule between me and my mother and my father as opposed to a group of sensory representations.

Once again we worked to reorganize that molecule into a more appropriate structure. *Organized in time and organized by a perceptual position,* because, again, it is sometimes difficult to distinguish what beliefs you have modeled from others from your own beliefs.

We separate and reorganize that relational molecule and go to a position outside that system to bring in the resources that allow the reorganization.

Finally, we worked with **a molecule made up of our own identity,** the structure of which will create either a positively or negatively reinforcing system. This forms a *synesthesia of self, a molecule of self.* We explored how to organize that system into the most appropriate and ecological set of relationships.

CLOSING MEDITATION

Find yourself once again in a relaxed position. Allowing your mind to shift gears, to change its mode of operation from inputting information to integrating and processing information.

Perhaps you can get an image of yourself as if you were floating above yourself. As you look down at yourself, perhaps you can begin to focus on a part of your face that you feel very comfortable with, a part that in some way defines some of who you are.

It might be your eyes, mouth, eyebrows, nose, chin, cheeks, forehead. Begin to focus on that place. Go closer and closer so that you begin to see that part of you at another level.

Perhaps in your mind you can magnify this enough so that you begin to see the pores in your skin and maybe the tiny hairs. You go closer and closer, magnifying more and more so that you see some of the cells that make up that skin. And closer, far within yourself so that you can see individual cells and the nuclei of the cells and even further, going into that nucleus, into the core of that cell, deeper, closer. You can even see the chromosomes that make that cell, embedded deep inside the nucleus. Those chromosomes that come from both your mother and father integrating together in an interacting relationship.

As you focus even closer on that chromosome perhaps you can begin to find the strands of DNA that carry your genetic code, and on into the amino acids that make up that DNA, and closer to the molecules that make up this very tiny part of you. Closer and deeper you can see the electrons encircling the nucleus of the atom. Now the atom is beginning to scatter around you, becoming larger and larger, so that you find yourself in a seeming infinite space in between the atoms.

Then you begin to come back up, seeing the electrons, the atoms forming together to make molecules, the molecules forming amino acids creating the genes and strands of DNA, the chromosomes and from that the individual cell, which forms with other cells to make pores of your skin. Then that skin becomes a part of your face, and as you look at your face you can continue to move further back to see your body and the bodies of the people next to you.

And you are going outside of the room to see that room in relation with the other rooms in the building. As the building grows small and distant, you see the other buildings in the city and the cars as if they were the cells of the city: all the way to the boundaries of the city, further to see the other cities. Further still you begin to see the edges of the country and the other countries surrounding it, the blue water of the ocean. Now you are going further, going up through the clouds watching the continents, the other bodies of water, and bodies of land get smaller below. Finally, you begin to see the edges of that blue ball, that blue jewel growing smaller and smaller. The other planets begin to appear all around, smaller and smaller until you can see them as if they were the atoms that made larger molecules.

Perhaps our own solar system is a tiny molecule in the body of God that makes us a part of a chromosome, a cell, a face.

As you hold in your mind all of these different levels it can be useful and interesting to remember that we do exist on all of these levels, perhaps as a hologram.

And if, as Einstein said, "The universe is a friendly place," then the things you have learned here will integrate themselves into you in the most comfortable and ecological way for you.

As you begin to sense the other people around you, the other identities, you can begin to come all the way back into this room. But hold on to a bit of that sense of that vast molecule of which we are a part.

I would like to thank you all for your participation, your questions, your energy, your beliefs; most importantly for your being you, for your identities. I shall see you sometime, if not in this universe then in some other I am sure.

Thank you and good-bye!

APPENDIX A

META PROGRAM PATTERNS

1. Orientation To Goals and Problems

a. Towards the Positive.
   Away From the Negative.

b. Match (Sort for *Similarities*).
   Mismatch (Sort for *Differences*).

c. **Thinking Style**
   Vision
   Action
   Logic
   Emotion

d. Hierarchy of **Criteria** (Values).
   Power (Control)
   Affiliation (Relationships)
   Achievement (Goals)

2. Orientation To Relationships

a. **Self** – 1st Position
   Other – 2nd Position
   Context – 3rd Position

b. External Behavior.
   Internal Response.

3. Orientation To Time:

a. Past – Remembered
   Present – External
   Future – Constructed

b. In Time (Associated)
   Through Time (Dissociated).

4. Orientation To Information Organization

a. Person – *Who*
   Information – *What*
   Place – *Where*
   Time – *When*
   Activity – *How*

b. **Chunk Size:**
   Large Chunks
   Small Chunks

APPENDIX B
PREDICATES AND EYE MOVEMENTS

Neuro-Linguistic Programming has identified a number of verbal and non-verbal indicators that may be used as clues to uncover pieces of someone's mental processes with or without their conscious cooperation.

1. Linguistic Clues

'Predicates' are words, such as verbs, adverbs and adjectives, which indicate actions or qualities as opposed to things. This type of language is typically selected at an unconscious level and thus reflects the underlying mental structure which produced them. Below is a list of commonly used predicates which indicate the use of one of the representational systems

VISUAL	AUDITORY	KINESTHETIC
"see"	*"hear"*	*"grasp"*
"look"	*"listen"*	*"touch"*
"sight"	*"sound"*	*"feeling"*
"clear"	*"resonant"*	*"sol;d"*
"bright"	*"loud"*	*"heavy"*
"picture"	*"word"*	*"handle"*
"hazy"	*'noisy"*	*"rough"*
"brings to light"	*"rings a bell"*	*"connects"*
"show"	*"tell"*	*"move"*

2. Eye Movements

Automatic, unconscious eye movements often accompany particular thought processes indicating the accessing of one of the representational systems. These eye positions can also stimulate access to and support activity in a particular sensory system as well. NLP has categorized these cues into the following pattern:

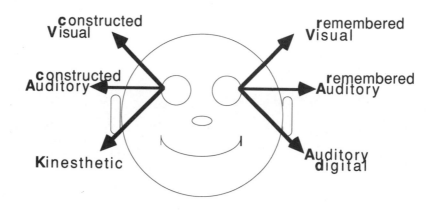

Eye Movement Chart

APPENDIX C:
Neurological Levels

I. Logical Levels

Gregory Bateson pointed out that in the processes of learning, change, and communication there were natural hierarchies of classification. The function of each level was to organize the information on the level below it, and the rules for changing something on one level were different from those for changing a lower level. Changing something on a lower level could, but would not necessarily, affect the upper levels; but changing something in the upper levels would necessarily change things on the lower levels in order to support the higher level change. Bateson noted that it was the confusion of logical levels that often created problems.

II. Logical Levels in NLP

In working with NLP, the following logical levels are the most basic and the most important to consider:

	Spiritual	Transmission
A.	Who I Am—Identity (Who)	Mission
B.	My Belief System— Values, Criteria (Why)	Permission & Motivation
C.	My Capabilities— States, Strategies (How)	Direction
D.	What I Do— Specific Behaviors (What)	Actions

E.　My Environment—External Context　　Reactions
　　　(Where, When)

III. Neuro-Logical Levels

These different levels each bring a deeper commitment of neurological 'circuitry' into action.

　　　Spiritual:　Holographic - Nervous system as a whole.

A.　Identity: Immune system and endocrine system - Deep life-sustaining functions.

B.　Beliefs: Autonomic nervous system (e.g. heart rate, pupil dilation, etc.) - Unconscious responses.

C.　Capabilities: Cortical systems - Semiconscious actions (eye movements, posture, etc.)

D.　Behaviors: Motor system (pyramidal and cerebellum) - Conscious actions

E.　Environment: Peripheral nervous system - Sensations and reflex reactions.

IV. Examples of Statements at the Different Logical Levels

The following statements indicate the different levels of response from a person who has discovered that he or she has cancer.

A.　Identity - I am a cancer victim.

B.　Belief - It is false hope not to accept the inevitable.

C.　Capability - I am not capable of keeping well.

D.　Specific Behavior - I have a tumor.

E. Environment - The cancer is attacking me.

The following statements indicate the different levels in some-one who is working toward a health goal.

A. Identity - I am a healthy person.

B. Belief - If I am healthy I can help others.

C. Capability - I know how to influence my health.

D. Specific Behavior - I can act healthy sometimes.

E. Environment - The medicine healed me.

The following statements indicate the different levels in some-one with a drinking problem.

A. Identity - I am an alcoholic and will always be an alcoholic.

B. Belief - I have to drink in order to stay calm and be normal.

C. Capability - I can't seem to control my drinking.

D. Specific Behavior - I had too much to drink at the party.

E. Environment - When I get around my friends I like a drink or two.

V. Types of Change in NLP at the Different Logical Levels.

A. Evolutionary Change - Change at the Identity level.

Change in mission and purpose.

B. Generative Changes - Change at the Belief and Capability levels.

Change in motivations, permission, and direction.

C.   Remedial Change - Change at the Behavior and Environmental levels.

Change in actions and reactions.

APPENDIX D

SUB-MODALITIES

VISUAL	AUDITORY	KINESTHETIC
BRIGHTNESS (dim-bright)	VOLUME (loud-soft)	INTENSITY (**strong**-weak)
SIZE	TONE	AREA
(large-small)	(bass-treble)	(large-small)
COLOR (black & white-color)	PITCH (high-low)	TEXTURE (rough-smooth)
MOVEMENT (fast-slow-still)	TEMPO (fast-slow)	DURATION (constant-intermittent)
DISTANCE (near-far)	DISTANCE (close-far)	TEMPERATURE (hot-cold)
FOCUS (clear-fuzzy)	RHYTHM	WEIGHT (**heavy**-light)
LOCATION	LOCATION	LOCATION
DEPTH (3D-flat)		

META-MODALITIES

ASSOCIATED-DISSOCIATED	WORDS-TONES	EMOTIONAL-TACTILE
INTERNAL-EXTERNAL	INTERNAL-EXTERNAL	INTERNAL-EXTERNAL

GLOSSARY OF NLP TERMINOLOGY

Accessing Cues   Subtle behaviors that will both help to trigger and indicate which representational system a person is using to think with. Typical types of accessing cues include eye movements, voice tone and tempo, body posture, gestures, and breathing patterns.

Anchoring   The process of associating an internal response with some external trigger (similar to classical conditioning) so that the response may be quickly, and sometimes covertly, reaccessed.

Auditory   Relating to hearing or the sense of hearing.

Behavior   The specific physical actions and reactions through which we interact with the people and environment around us.

Behavioral Flexibility   The ability to vary one's own behavior in order to elicit or secure a response from another person.

Beliefs   Closely held generalizations about (1) cause, (2) meaning, and (3) boundaries in the (a) world around us, (b) our behavior, (c) our capabilities, and (d) our identities. Beliefs function at a different level than concrete reality and serve to guide and interpret our perceptions of reality, often by connecting them to our criteria or value systems. Beliefs are notoriously difficult to change through typical rules of logic or rational thinking.

Calibration   The process of learning to read another person's unconscious, non-verbal responses in an ongoing interaction by pairing observable behavioral cues with a specific internal response.

Calibrated Loop Unconscious pattern of communication in which behavioral cues of one person trigger specific responses from another person in an ongoing interaction.

Capability Mastery over an entire class of behavior—knowing how to do something. Capabilities come from the development of a mental map that allows us to select and organize groups of individual behaviors. In NLP these mental maps take the form of cognitive strategies and meta-programs.

Chunking Organizing or breaking down some experience into bigger or smaller pieces. Chunking up involves moving to a larger, more abstract level of information. Chunking down involves moving to a more specific and concrete level of information. Chunking laterally involves finding other examples at the same level of information.

Congruence When all of a person's internal beliefs, strategies, and behaviors are fully in agreement and oriented toward securing a desired outcome.

Context The framework surrounding a particular event. This framework will often determine how a particular experience or event is interpreted.

Criteria The values or standards a person uses to make decisions and judgments.

Deep Structure The sensory maps (both conscious and unconscious) that people use to organize and guide their behavior.

Environment The external context in which our behavior takes place. Our environment is that which we perceive as being "outside" of us. It is not part of our behavior but is rather something we must react to.

Four Tuple (or 4-tuple) A shorthand method used to notate the structure of any particular experience. The concept of the four tuple maintains that any experience must be composed of some combination of the four primary representational classes—<A,V,K,O>—where A = auditory, V = visual, K = kinesthetic, and O = olfactory/gustatory.

Future Pacing The process of mentally rehearsing oneself through some future situation in order to help ensure that the desired behavior will occur naturally and automatically.

Gustatory Relating to taste or the sense of taste.

Identity Our sense of who we are. Our sense of identity organizes our beliefs, capabilities, and behaviors into a single system.

Installation The process of facilitating the acquisition of a new strategy or behavior. A new strategy may be installed through some combination of anchoring, accessing cues, metaphor, and future pacing.

Kinesthetic Relating to body sensations. In NLP the term kinesthetic is used to encompass all kinds of feelings including tactile, visceral, and emotional.

Logical Levels An internal hierarchy in which each level is progressively more psychologically encompassing and impactful. In order of importance (from high to low) these levels include (1) identity, (2) beliefs, (3) capabilities, (4) behavior, and (5) environment.

Meta Model A model developed by John Grinder and Richard Bandler that identifies categories of language patterns that can be problematic or ambiguous.

Meta Program A level of mental programming that determines how we sort, orient to, and chunk our experiences. Our meta programs are more abstract than our specific strategies for thinking and define our general approach to a particular issue rather than the details of our thinking process.

Metaphor   The process of thinking about one situation or phenomenon as something else, i.e., stories, parables, and analogies.

Modeling   The process of observing and mapping the successful behaviors of other people.

Neuro-Linguistic Programming (NLP)   A behavioral model and set of explicit skills and techniques founded by John Grinder and Richard Bandler in 1975. Defined as the study of the structure of subjective experience. NLP studies the patterns or "programming" created by the interaction among the brain (neuro), language (linguistic), and the body that produce both effective and ineffective behavior. The skills and techniques were derived by observing the patterns of excellence in experts from diverse fields of professional communication, including psychotherapy, business, hypnosis, law, and education.

Olfactory   Relating to smell or the sense of smell.

Outcomes   Goals or desired states that a person or organization aspires to achieve.

Pacing   A method used by communicators to quickly establish rapport by matching certain aspects of their behavior to those of the person with whom they are communicating—a matching or mirroring of behavior.

Parts   A metaphorical way of talking about independent programs and strategies of behavior. Programs or "parts" will often develop a persona that becomes one of their identifying features.

Position   A particular perspective or point of view. In NLP there are three basic positions one can take in perceiving a particular experience. First position involves experiencing something through our own eyes associated in a first person point of view. Second position involves experiencing something as if we were in another person's shoes. Third position involves standing back and perceiving the relationship between ourselves and others from a dissociated perspective.

Predicates   Process words (like verbs, adverbs, and adjectives) that a person selects to describe a subject. Predicates are used in NLP to identify which representational system a person is using to process information.

Quotes   A pattern in which a message that you want to deliver can be embedded in quotations, as if someone else had stated the message.

Rapport   The establishment of trust, harmony, and cooperation in a relationship.

Reframing   A process used in NLP through which a problematic behavior is separated from the positive intention of the internal program or "part" that is responsible for the behavior. New choices of behavior are established by having the part responsible for the old behavior take responsibility for implementing other behaviors that satisfy the same positive intention but don't have the problematic byproducts.

Representational Systems   The five senses: seeing, hearing, touching (feeling), smelling, and tasting.

Representational System Primacy   Where an individual systematically uses one sense over the others to process and organize his or her experience. Primary representational system will determine many personality traits as well as learning capabilities.

Secondary Gain   Where some seemingly negative or problematic behavior actually carries out some positive function at some other level. For example, smoking may help a person to relax or help them fit a particular self image.

State   The total ongoing mental and physical conditions from which a person is acting.

Strategy   A set of explicit mental and behavioral steps used to achieve a specific outcome. In NLP, the most important aspect of a strategy is the representational systems used to carry out the specific steps.

Sub-Modalities   The special sensory qualities perceived by each of the senses. For example, visual sub-modalities include color, shape, movement, brightness, depth, etc., auditory sub-modalities include volume, pitch, tempo, etc., and kinesthetic sub-modalities include pressure, temperature, texture, location, etc.

Surface Structure   The words or language used to describe or stand for the actual primary sensory representations stored in the brain.

Synesthesia   The process of overlap between representational systems, characterized by phenomena like see-feel circuits, in which a person derives feelings for what he sees, and hear-feel circuits, in which a person gets feelings from what they hear. Any two sensory modalities may be linked together.

T.O.T.E.   Developed by Miller, Galanter and Pribram, the term stands for the sequence Test-Operate-Test-Exit, which describes the basic feedback loop used to guide all behavior.

Transderivational Search   The process of searching back through one's stored memories and mental representations to find the reference experience from which a current behavior or response was derived.

Translating   The process of rephrasing words from one type of representational system predicates to another.

Utilization   A technique in which a specific strategy sequence or pattern of behavior is paced or matched in order to influence another's response.

Visual   Relating to sight or the sense of sight.

Well-Formedness Conditions   The set of conditions something must satisfy in order to produce an effective and ecological outcome. In NLP a particular goal is well-formed if it
can be: (1) stated in positive terms, (2) defined and evaluated
according to sensory based evidence, (3) initiated and main-
tained by the person who desires the goal, (4) made to preserve the positive byproducts of the present state, and
(5) appropriately contextualized to fit the external ecology.